**DATE DUE**

| | | | |
|---|---|---|---|
| | | | |
| | | | |
| | | | |
| | | | |
| | | | |
| | | | |
| | | | |
| | | | |
| | | | |
| | | | |
| | | | |

# CULTURES OF AMERICA

# GREEK AMERICANS

By David Phillips and Steven Ferry

**BENCHMARK BOOKS**

MARSHALL CAVENDISH

**Benchmark Books**
Marshall Cavendish Corporation
99 White Plains Road
Tarrytown, New York 10591-9001, U.S.A.

© Marshall Cavendish Corporation, 1996

Edited, designed, and produced by Water Buffalo Books, Milwaukee

The authors and editors gratefully acknowledge the following for their help in the creation of this book: Maria Pantelias, Father Tryfon Theophilopoulos, John Lulias, John Eigner, Nick Toth, George Katsaros, and the Pappas family.

**Picture Credits:** Courtesy of John and Helen Arapis: 58; Sabine Beaupré 1995: 7, 17; © The Bettmann Archive: 9, 13, 25, 26; © Steven Ferry: Cover, 1, 30, 32, 33, 34, 36, 38, 39, 40, 41, 42, 43 (bottom), 44, 45, 47, 48, 49, 50, 51, 52, 53 (both), 54, 55, 57 (both), 59, 60, 62, 63, 64, 70, 71; © Hazel Hankin: 4, 28, 61; Courtesy of Argiro Mavrikis: 35; Courtesy of Konstantinos Mavrikis: 43 (top); © Reuters/Bettmann: 68; © Springer/Bettmann Film Archive: 72 (bottom); © M. Thonig/H. Armstrong Roberts: 6; Courtesy of Theonie and Panayiota Tsigistras: 5, 31; © UPI/Bettmann: 10, 12, 16, 19, 22, 23, 65, 66, 67, 69, 72 (top), 73, 74, 75

**Library of Congress Cataloging-in-Publication Data**

Ferry, Steven.
    Greek Americans / by Steven Ferry and David Phillips.
        p.    cm. -- (Cultures of America)
    Includes bibliographical references and index.
    Summary: Provides a history of Greek immigration to the United States and discusses Greek customs and contributions to American culture.
    ISBN 0-7614-0161-X (lib. bdg.)
    1. Greek Americans--Juvenile literature. [1. Greek Americans.] I. Phillips, David, 1954 Apr. 24- II. Title. III. Series.
    E184.G7G693        1995
    973'.0489--dc20                                                    95-11034
                                                                         CIP
                                                                         AC

To PS – MS

Printed in Malaysia
Bound in the U.S.A.

# CONTENTS

# INTRODUCTION

Few countries can claim as much credit as Greece for influencing the direction of American culture. Almost every subject taught in school today was first developed by the Greeks. Many parts of our lives, from the U.S. Constitution to nuclear energy, have their roots in the early theories and discoveries of the ancient Greeks.

The Greeks who came knocking at America's doors in the 1880s, however, were not the ancient Greeks. These were a very different people, mostly uneducated farmers looking for jobs so that they could return home with pockets full of money. The work was hard and they faced discrimination, but they quickly learned the language and customs and established themselves in businesses. Many of them never returned home, preferring to stay in the Greek communities they established in the United States.

Over the last century, these Greek Americans have become a valuable part of American society. Because they still care deeply about their homeland, they have also managed to preserve their Greek heritage. This book is the story of their arrival and progress in this country and a description of life for Greek Americans today.

A small village near Andritsena, in the Peloponnesos region of Greece. The mountainous land that covers much of the country has made farming difficult for centuries.

# LEAVING A HOMELAND
## WE'LL BE BACK

"**W**e went to bed without any food last night," said Theo, brushing a fly out of his face. It was another hot, boring day. "Baba got mad at Maki for throwing stones at Alevizos's sheep." Life for two young boys in a Greek village 150 years ago offered few opportunities for recreation, and discipline was often strict.

"There is nothing else to do in the village," Evangelos answered after a long pause.

Theo laughed. "Maybe if Baba's crops grew," he said, "we could have one of Alevizos's sheep for dinner, instead of just bread."

Evangelos didn't seem to hear. Instead, he mumbled to himself, "Baba swears the rains will start and the grapes will grow again. How does he know?" There had been no rain for months, and the crops were in danger of dying.

"Good question; he doesn't," answered Theo. "And if the tax collector comes again, we'll all be in trouble."

Evangelos looked at Theo, the thought of the tax collector's last visit fresh in his mind. They had lost everything when he came, except the house and the fields. Even the beds had been taken.

Suddenly, Evangelos stood up and looked his cousin straight in the eye. He took his hands and said, "Swear with me,

Theo, that we'll do something to help our families? We have to leave and find work somewhere, earn money so we don't have to live like this anymore."

"What are we going to do? All we know is farming, and there's no better place to do it than right here!" yelled Theo, suddenly angered by his cousin's outburst.

Evangelos sat down again, silent.

"I'll tell you one thing," said Theo, as he threw a stone at one of Alevizos's sheep, "If Yaya says one more thing about how the Turks took her eldest son, I *will* leave!" Every day for the last thirty-five years, his grandmother, or *yaya*, had mentioned how her eighteen-year-old son had been taken

**Greeks immigrated to America from many different regions of Greece, bringing with them their local traditions and loyalties.**

## FOREIGN RULE AND THE IMPORTANCE OF THE CHURCH

Although the Greeks were leaders in many fields of knowledge twenty-five hundred years ago, their society fell behind other European countries in 1453, when they were conquered by the Turks. Turkey and Greece lie next to each other at the eastern end of the Mediterranean Sea. They have been fighting each other ever since the Turks took control of a part of Greece — Constantinople — six hundred years ago. Their differences began, however, after the Greeks became Christians in the first century A.D. and seven hundred years later the Turks became Muslims.

In 1453, the Turks got the upper hand, ruling the whole of Greece for the next four hundred years. During this time, they suppressed the Greek culture, knowledge, and religion. They taxed Greeks heavily and took

many of their young boys away to fight in the Turkish army. They would not allow the Greeks to practice their customs, to meet except for religious reasons, or to educate their children. The Turks controlled Greek lives to prevent them from organizing and resisting Turkish rule.

One important way the Greeks kept their language, religion, and hopes alive throughout this difficult period was through regular visits to their Greek Orthodox churches. There, the priests, whom the Turks had put in charge of running the community, secretly let them talk about and practice their customs and language. It was Archbishop Germanos who eventually started the Greek war of independence from the Turks in 1832. The church has therefore always been especially important to Greeks.

away by the Turkish rulers to fight in their army and had died in some distant battle.

Evangelos didn't say anything. Instead, he started to hum a song he had heard recently. Pretty soon, Theo was joining in. Then, the words came to them, and they sang as loudly as they could at the hillside where Alevizos's sheep grazed: "Mother, I want to go to foreign lands. To foreign lands I must go."

### An Undeveloped Country in Modern Europe

After four hundred years of Turkish rule, the Greece of 1850 looked little different than the Greece of 1450. While European countries had developed industries and built machines and factories, the Turks had not industrialized and therefore did not encourage or permit the Greeks to do so either.

When the Greeks finally tried to modernize, they faced real problems. Their country had almost no natural resources. There were few minerals or coal fields to mine or trees to harvest. The country had no vast, rolling plains to graze cattle; nor were there plentiful rivers to help irrigate crops. Communication and trade were difficult because there were few roads over the mountains that divided the country.

Most Greeks were uneducated because there were almost no schools for them to attend. Education had not been allowed by the Turks, so parents secretly taught their young children in caves, with few books or other learning tools available. Without any other training or jobs available, almost everyone worked on farms, using the techniques and tools of their ancestors. They tried to support themselves on rocky and mountain-

In this photo taken in the late 1800s or early 1900s, a Greek woman takes caskets of vinegar to the market, where she will sell them to help support her family. After centuries of foreign rule, Greece did not become industrialized as quickly as other European nations.

ous land, but it was hard. Families shared small houses, sometimes a dozen people in one or two rooms, and often went hungry.

## Life in the Home

Greeks believed that the family was all-important, and the husband was the absolute head. His job was to support the family and make major decisions. His word was law. He controlled the finances and would not consult with his wife at all on questions of money, unless he wanted to sell the house. In that case, he would ask her first, as it was often her house, given to the couple by her family as a dowry when they married. (A dowry is money or property which, in some countries, a woman brings to her husband when she marries him.)

The wife's duties were in the home: cooking, looking after the children, and seeing that everything ran smoothly in the house. As the saying went, "Without a woman, there is no house."

## Bread and Wine on the Table

The Greeks had many centuries to develop the best ways of cooking the food they had available. They would often have soup, because it made a little go far: white bean, lentil, lamb, fish, and lemon and chicken, to name a few. They made feta cheese from the milk of goats and sheep, and they ate lamb and goat meat. Surrounded as they were by the sea, they often ate seafood, including octopus and squid, seasoned with fresh herbs that grew wild.

Unmarried Greek women dancing in 1920. While most women were were not allowed to date, they still had to look their best to attract the attention of the families of potential husbands.

Greek salads were popular in the summer, served in large wooden bowls with plates of bread, cheese, and olives. The family sat on the floor or on small stools, with the food on a small round table in front of them. The family members helped themselves, usually using their fingers.

Sometimes little food was available, and mothers would have to find whatever they could to feed their families. One common dish in hard times was wild dandelion greens, boiled and flavored with olive oil and lemon. That would be a main course, served with chunks of bread.

Each family made its own wines and enjoyed them at home. They had retsina (a white wine flavored with pine tree sap), sweet red wine, and ouzo (a drink flavored with anise, giving it a taste similar to licorice), which they often drank at celebrations.

## Dating, Marriage, and Family

Traditionally, Greek parents arranged marriages for their children without even asking them. Dating and romantic love were considered too stressful for the children and upsetting for their families. It was much easier for the parents to arrange everything, sometimes with the help of a matchmaker. Matchmakers were usually older women who would bring the fathers of two families together to decide if their son and daughter should marry and how much the dowry would be. This custom enabled parents to control their own children and determine whom they married.

For Greeks, the family did not just mean father, mother, and the children. It also meant grandparents, aunts, uncles, cousins, nephews, and nieces. The interests of one member were the interests of the whole family. If one family member was in trouble, the whole family felt threatened, and they all helped out.

Each family wanted three things: first, to have as many members as possible, so they would have greater influence in running the village; second, to have a well-run house with the father firmly in charge; and third, to own as much land as possible to support all the relatives. In those days, aging parents and grandparents were looked after at home.

Being part of such a large family provided security for individuals in facing the challenges of life. Another vital support for individuals and family alike was the Greek Orthodox Church.

## Faith, Philosophy, and Superstitions

The Greeks were deeply religious people who had been closely involved with their church since the early days of Christianity. Even centuries of control and abuse by Muslim Turks had not shaken their belief in Christianity.

The Greeks also believed in fate, an idea that was common in the Muslim world, too. They believed that whether someone lived or died, or whether some action succeeded or failed, was a matter of fate and out of their control.

Greeks had superstitious beliefs as well. Some people, for instance, were thought to have the "evil eye," which was the power to harm others just by looking at them or by putting curses on them. The way the Greeks protected themselves from this evil was by praying and going through certain rituals. If a baby was threatened, for instance, the mother could protect it by saying a prayer, rubbing its stomach, wrapping it in a special blanket, and then pretending to spit at the baby three times. Some people were known to have powerful prayers to overcome the evil eye, and they would be asked for help if needed.

## Social Life

While the Greeks took their faith and beliefs very seriously, they were also a fun-loving people and enjoyed their social life and activities. When not working, men spent their free time at "men only" cafes, where they talked while smoking Turkish

*narghiles* (pronounced NAR-gi-lees), tobacco pipes that filtered the smoke through a bowl of water. Or they would sit quietly, drinking strong coffee and fingering small strings of beads made of amber (yellow tree sap that has hardened with age, becoming a fossil). Sometimes they would watch silhouette plays, much like puppet shows, or dance together.

The women would get together to embroider and talk but rarely went to public places. Children would use their imaginations to play games. They also played with homemade toys, such as a doll made of an old sock stuffed with straw and with eyes embroidered on its face. They may not have had much, but they didn't need much to enjoy themselves.

## Celebrating with Song and Dance

The whole community would get together to sing and dance during weddings, religious festivals, and other celebrations. Vases as old as twenty-five hundred years show paintings of Greek dancers doing the same basic dances Greeks performed in 1850. The songs, dances, and even techniques for making musical instruments were successfully passed on from father to son and mother to daughter for centuries.

During the Turkish occupation from the 1400s to the 1800s, the only times the Greeks could openly express their feelings and continue their cultural traditions were when they danced and sang at religious celebrations. After the Turks left, Greeks danced whenever there was something to celebrate. People would even do small dance steps at work, at home, and in cafes. Dances were not performed only on stage or at formal celebrations; they were a way of expressing oneself throughout the day.

Greek women perform a *syrtos*, or slow dance, in the village square around 1920. Some dances involved only women or men, and others included both men and women.

There were two types of Greek dance: the *syrtos*, which was slow and dragging as the dancers held tightly onto each other's arms and were led in a line by a dancer twirling a handkerchief. The other type was the *pedektos*, in which dancers hopped. Each region developed its own version of each dance, so there were hundreds of traditional dances. The *sousta*, for instance, was a lively version of the pedektos dance performed mainly in Crete (a Greek island south of the mainland) and the Greek Dodecanese islands (near the Turkish coast). This dance was more undulating (moving up and down like a wave) than hopping. The men had the lead role and danced complicated steps, which they often made up as they went along. As women wore large dresses made of heavy cloth and weighing up to thirty pounds, they specialized in the smoother syrtos dances.

Women took great pride in the costumes and clothes that they made. A girl, for instance, would sew and embroider her own clothes from the age of seven. Girls wore colorful dresses and aprons with patterns on

## A DANCE CALLED *MECHANIKOS*

The Kalymnians, people from the Greek island of Kalymnos, made a living diving for sponges. They developed a new version of the sousta dance, which they called the *mechanikos*, meaning "mechanical." The dance showed a sponge diver coming up from the deep, wearing the diving suit that had just been invented. The dancers' motions imitated divers with "the bends" (paralyzing cramps caused by rising to the surface too fast).

them that indicated which area and family they were from and whether they were married. They also sewed for the menfolk, who wore vests, leggings, and kilts, or short skirts, that also gave information about the wearer. The embroidery showed, for instance, whether a man was married, what his job was, and whether he had fought in any wars. Women made special dancing costumes that emphasized the movements of the dancers, forming shapes and patterns as the cloth flowed and bounced.

Although each area in Greece had its own preferred instrument, the basic orchestra for both song and dance usually included a clarinet, a violin, a lute, and a *santouri,* a wooden stringed instrument similar to a dulcimer. Musicians also sometimes used drums or tambourines or both to keep rhythm, but usually only when playing outside as they were so loud. Greek folk music was hard to perform for musicians trained in Western European musical traditions. The scales were unusual, the rhythms were more complex, and there was rarely any harmony as all of the instruments played the same tune.

Although the Greeks took every opportunity to spice their lives with dance and song, they could not avoid the problems they were facing at the end of the 1800s.

This young woman is wearing a costume peculiar to Kynouria, in the state of Arcadia in Peloponnesos. At that time, women made their dresses by hand over a long period of time.

## Natural Disasters and Political Unrest

Greeks faced plenty of hardship in the nineteenth century. Crop failures, droughts, and earthquakes were natural catastrophes that could wipe out a whole year's work, and

## MUSICAL INSTRUMENTS OF ANCIENT GREECE

The instruments played by most Greeks in the 1800s were not the same as those first used in Greece. In the two thousand years the Greeks had been keeping track of their history, some things had changed. For instance, the modern clarinet had replaced the shepherd's pipe, and the violin had replaced the lyre (a small, harplike instrument). Even so, some areas still used the ancient instruments. Pipes and drums were quite common throughout Greece, and the lyre, which had developed into a narrow violin, was played in Crete. In Macedonia, the bag pipe could still be heard.

there were also artificial problems to deal with. The cost of food and other items kept increasing. Greece was at war with neighboring countries, and the government had to look after both native Greeks and refugees fleeing to Greece to escape the fighting. It was hard for businesses and people to prosper in such a dangerous environment.

In addition to external problems, certain beliefs at the core of Greek society did little to help people work together to resolve common problems. For example, the Greeks believed strongly in *philotimo,* a code of conduct that included demanding respect for oneself and one's family, defending one's honor, and doing one's duty. If a distant family member were insulted, for instance, it was the duty of all the men in the family to punish the offender and preserve the family honor.

Unfortunately for the Greeks, with this idea of honor came an attitude: that a man always had to have the upper hand. He had to outtalk and outdo all the others, so that he would not appear inferior. Quick-tempered, he would not follow orders but preferred to do things his own way. Four hundred years of following hated Turkish orders only strengthened this attitude among Greek men.

When the Greeks finally gained their freedom, philotimo made it even harder for them to work together to modernize their country. Many government officials, for instance, devoted more effort to arguing with each other than trying to solve the country's problems.

## Why Greeks Left Their Homeland

Throughout the nineteenth century, the Greeks tried to modernize their country and raise their standard of living, but by the last quarter of the 1800s, things took a turn for the worse. Greeks had grown olives for centuries but had destroyed many of the trees and planted vineyards in their place. These vineyards produced currants, small raisins used in baking, which Greek farmers sold mostly in France. They managed to make ends meet with this crop for a while. Then, to protect its own farmers, the French government placed a heavy tax on Greek currants so that they would be too expensive to import into France. Unable to sell their fruit abroad, the Greek farmers and their families ran out of money. It was only then that the Greeks were forced to leave the country to earn the cash they needed to survive.

While they had never known anything but their large families and home villages with their own religion and customs, Greek men knew that they were not thriving. They had to change something. So when friends, family members, or strangers visited

### PHILOTIMO IN A NEW SETTING

The attitude calling for the defense of honor and settling of scores called *philotimo* (pronounced fee-LOT-eemo) seems alive and well in modern-day Greece. In 1979, Greeks experienced 195 deaths on the road for every one hundred thousand cars (in the U.S., the figure is three in every hundred thousand). According to the Hellenic Automobile and Touring Club of Greece, "Greek drivers have the mistaken idea that everyone is out to challenge and humiliate them and, therefore, must be defeated."

## MONEY FOR SISTERS AND FAMILIES

In addition to providing for their families, Greek men who emigrated wanted to earn money for another reason: They had to provide dowries for their sisters. In the nineteenth century, a girl or woman had to contribute money and a house or furniture to her future husband if she wanted to marry. These contributions were called dowries.

Wives in Greece stayed at home and so did not earn any money. Providing a dowry,

therefore, gave the husband a head start in setting up the household. It was a matter of honor that fathers and brothers provide a dowry.

The husband who received the dowry could do whatever he wanted with the money he was given. Sometimes, he would give it to his sister for her dowry. And her husband might do the same with his sister. So the money might never be spent, but passed from one husband to another.

---

talking about the opportunities in the United States, they felt that they really had no choice. They may have wanted to stay, but they had to go for the sake of family honor and survival.

The men planned to work hard and send home most of the money they earned. When they had earned their fortunes, these fathers and brothers aimed to return to the families, villages, and country they loved.

### Making a Fortune in America

Young men wondering where they could earn the money their families needed soon heard an answer: "You can make more money in America than you ever will at home." So many Greek men, speaking only Greek

and knowing only how to farm, left their villages for a country thousands of miles away.

The Greek government encouraged young men to emigrate when it recognized how much money was being sent back from the States. Life was getting much easier in the villages that sent the most men. There was enough good food to eat, buildings were improved, families paid off their debts, and people could buy the things they wanted.

In the last decades of the nineteenth century, 18,000 Greeks emigrated to the United States. In the first decades of the twentieth century, another 350,000 followed. By 1925, one in every four Greek men between the ages of fifteen and forty-five had gone to the United States

---

## WHY AMERICA?

Although Greeks had gone to various countries to seek their fortunes, it was not until a young man named Christos Tsakonas returned from the United States in 1875 that America became a popular destination for emigrating Greek farmers. Christos went to the States when he was twenty-five and

returned to Sparta two years later. He persuaded five of his friends to go to the U.S. with him, and they settled in Chicago, selling fruit on the streets. They all liked enough of what they saw to try to convince more of their friends to emigrate, and so the word spread: "Come to America and make your fortune!"

These women are among three hundred "picture" brides who arrived in New York harbor by ship in January 1921. Each carries a picture of the man she intends to marry, whom she has never met. The men, many of whom have lived in the United States for several years, are on the pier waiting for their new wives and have brought pictures of the women they have arranged to marry.

# CHAPTER TWO

# LIFE IN A NEW LAND
## THE LONG ROAD TO SUCCESS

**E**vangelos hugged his mother one last time outside the small farmhouse he had called home for twenty years. She shouldn't cry, he thought. He whispered in her ear, "I promise to write as soon as I arrive in America. I will send hundreds of drachmas so my sister can afford to marry. You shall see."

He turned from his friends and walked away from the small village in Sparta, the region in southern Greece where he had lived all his life. He headed toward the coast, where the ship was waiting. The trip lasted a month and three days. He managed to tolerate the stink and the cramped quarters — three hundred people crammed into an area at the bottom of the ship so small that it was hard to move, let alone think.

Evangelos needed to think, for there was something troubling him. He was bound for the United States, where jobs were available and a man could make his way. But would he be sent home? All his life, his eyes had bothered him. "If the doctors in their white coats on Ellis Island

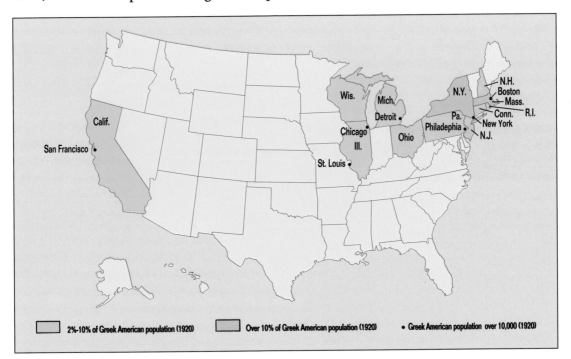

2%-10% of Greek American population (1920)    Over 10% of Greek American population (1920)    • Greek American population over 10,000 (1920)

**The earliest Greek immigrants formed communities in many U.S. cities, especially in and around New York and Boston. By the 1920s, they had fanned out across the nation, with their greatest numbers in the Northeast and upper Midwest.**

examine your eyes, they will not let you through," his cousin in America had written him. People coming to the United States had to pass a health exam and be found fit and well. But work at home had been so hard to find, Evangelos had to try at least. He had borrowed money for this trip; would it all be thrown away? He had to work out some plan before the ship arrived in the U.S.

The immigrants let out a cheer when they saw the Statue of Liberty. Here was hope, freedom in sight! When the ship docked at Ellis Island, the first stop for immigrants to the United States, it was raining and cold. Here, Evangelos found hundreds of men, women, and children, all speaking peculiar languages, packed into the registry room. There, they waited patiently to see the doctor, the last barrier before being allowed into the United States. Every now and then, a man would be led back, chalk marks on his coat showing he had failed the medical examination.

Evangelos's heart sank as the man in front of him was sent through to waiting relatives. Now was the moment of truth, and

## FEW GREEKS CAME TO AMERICA IN THE EARLY DAYS

Between 1847 and 1864, while hundreds of thousands of other Europeans immigrated to America, only seventy-seven Greeks arrived. In 1860, records showed only two Greeks in Texas and one in New Mexico. Even by 1890, there were only about two hundred Greeks in all the western states, most of them running saloons and grocery stores. It was not until the 1890s that the mass exodus of farmers like Evangelos arrived.

Evangelos felt the shame of failing already beginning to overwhelm him. The doctor turned mechanically toward Evangelos, one more immigrant to check among so many.

Then he heard a voice shouting from the far end of the hall. "Doctor, your attention please, this man has collapsed."

Evangelos did not understand what the big American official was calling out, but slowly it dawned on him that the doctor was no longer standing in front of him. Without thinking, he turned and ran as fast as his legs would carry him through the gate, down a passageway, and to freedom. He stood outside in the rain, raised his arms to the sky, and yelled with joy.

## Making a Living — Where to Start?

Evangelos's first priority on arriving in the States was to find his cousin, Konstantinos, who lived in Chicago. He hoped to find a job as a busboy or waiter in the same restaurant where his cousin worked. Maybe he would be the dishwasher.

Evangelos was lucky because he had someone to turn to. A friend he had made on the ship, Theano, had no contacts and planned to go to New England. He had been told work could be found there in a mill or factory making shoes, hats, or cloth. Others had spoken of trying their luck in the West, working in a mine or on the railroads. Theano didn't want to be a bootblack (shoeshine boy) or peddler on the streets, like some of his fellow travelers, and he didn't know how to dive for sponges, which is what three brothers from Salonica hoped to do in Florida.

The Greek men had spent the long, hot days on the boat boasting about the beauty of their women, the influence of their families, and the size of their villages. They had been less certain, though, talking about their futures in the United States. With the exception of the sponge divers, they had all been farmers back home. But these days, it seemed, the money was not on farms. And unlike the Greek farms they knew, American farms were isolated and lonely places to work. They had all agreed that they would rather live in towns and cities, with other Greeks for friends. They would be in the States for only a few years, so why get tied up in a farm? Where would they find the money to buy land, anyway?

## Finding Work

Life in the United States was not easy for Greek immigrants once they arrived. They could only work for other Greeks because Americans seldom offered them jobs. If the boss were a stranger, he would sometimes not pay for the work done. If the boss were a relative, life was easy, but there was always the worry that he would bring a closer relative over from Greece to do the job instead. In Greece, family always comes first.

Like many immigrants, the Greeks used the Italian *padrone* system to find jobs. This meant that a stranger, called a padrone (Italian for "boss"), would pay for people to come to the United States, find them a job, and then take most of their money. With

This photo, taken in 1939 in Tarpon Springs, Florida, features a sponge diver's suit blown up more than usual to show how airtight the suit is. Normally, the stone around the diver's neck, as well as the heavy helmet and boots, help the diver stay at the bottom where the sponges grow.

little money of their own, these boys and men were forced to live in room provided by the padrone, sleeping like sardines on the floor and eating nothing but bean soup every day. Many Greeks returned home, feeling, as one of them put it, that they would

## THE FIRST GREEKS IN AMERICA

John Griego, a Greek, is said to have sailed with Christopher Columbus in 1492. But the first record we have of a Greek setting foot on American soil was some thirty years later, in 1528. Don Teodoro, a Greek, was on a Spanish ship that anchored off Pensacola, Florida. The captain needed fresh water, and the Native Americans there agreed to let his men have some, as long as he left a hostage. Don Teodoro volunteered to be the hostage. He was never seen again. Maybe he was killed; maybe he liked what he found and decided to stay.

Several hundred years later, in the 1770s, the first large band of Greeks, four hundred, landed in New Smyrna, Florida. They expect- ed to find fields to farm; instead, they found swamps and mosquitoes. They were badly treated by their "employer," an Englishman who had brought them over with false promises and who would have them whipped if they did not do what he wanted. Those who did not die of malaria eventually left and went north to St. Augustine, Florida. There they settled successfully as merchants and established the first Greek Orthodox chapel in the Americas. The oldest wooden school- house in America was also founded at this time by John Giannopoulos, a Greek immi- grant, in his own home. It is still standing today and was recently made into a shrine in honor of this first band of Greek Americans.

"rather eat bread and onions" than work like slaves fifteen hours a day for no return.

## Much Hardship, Little Money

Like Evangelos, most of the Greek immi- grants arriving in the United States were young men who wanted to make money and send it back home, mainly for their sisters' dowries. Keeping little of their hard-earned wages for themselves, they often lived lives of hardship as a result. These young men would often delay their own marriage plans until they had taken care of their sisters.

While working as manual laborers in the cities during the beginning of the century, some immigrants slept on floors or tables at work to avoid spending money on rent. Others slept on beds in large rooms with several other Greeks. One boy in New York City shared such a room with six men and the seven peanut-vending wagons they used in their work during the day.

The railroad workers and miners on the West Coast slept in damp tents and crowded shacks. They received poor food and med- ical care. Lazy doctors, for instance, would just cut off an injured leg or arm, instead of treating it properly so it could heal. The men worked very long hours in dangerous conditions. Close to two hundred Greek miners were killed in just three accidents between 1913 and 1924.

Living conditions for the early immi- grants were not good. But with the Greek sense of pride, perhaps their worst experi- ence was the discrimination they met.

## Discrimination

By 1900, enough Greeks had arrived in the United States to attract attention. The impression they gave Americans was not good. Although they were friendly, they kept mainly to the company of other Greeks and, it seemed, always spoke loudly and in their own language. They spent little money on themselves and their homes, so they looked poor. They had no women to care for their clothes after a day on a filthy job, so they were often dirty, too. They were therefore considered different and were discriminated against. One fourteen-year-old street vendor in New York City described how he was beaten up regularly on the streets just for being Greek.

Life in the United States turned pretty unpleasant for most Greeks in the first quarter of the century. In South Omaha, Nebraska, mob violence broke out in February 1909. One Sunday morning, a crowd smashed and burned down the homes and shops of over one thousand Greeks, forcing them all to run for their lives and leave the state. The mob was angry at Greeks who had been brought to town to replace striking workers at factories that paid low wages. At the same time, townspeople feared the competition to their businesses from the forty or more successful grocery stores that other hard-working Greeks had opened in town.

Not all Greek communities had trouble, though. In Spartanburg, South Carolina, Nicholas Trakas opened a candy store. Many other Greeks from his native Sparta followed him. They followed his example, avoided unskilled or menial jobs, and jumped straight into small business ownership. Unlike the Greeks working in the mines and factories elsewhere in the United States, who were unable to afford good clothes or keep themselves clean on their dirty jobs, the Greek shop owners in Spartanburg were able to dress well and stay clean. Their appearance, therefore, appealed to the middle-class values of the other Spartanburg residents. As more Greeks arrived, they settled in different parts of the town

## PREJUDICE MAKES LIFE DIFFICULT

In Montana, a citizen's committee was formed in 1909 to drive all Greeks out of the state because people there did not like the way the Greeks lived. By 1921, prejudice against immigrants in general had reached such a level that the U.S. government passed the Johnson Act, limiting the number of immigrants allowed into the United States each year. For Greeks, this meant only one hundred immigrants could leave Greece for America every year.

rather than forming a large, concentrated group of strangers. Greeks contributed, especially financially, to local community projects and did not take jobs away from people who had lived there longer. The townsfolk accepted them as fellow citizens.

Another area where Greeks experienced little discrimination was Tarpon Springs, on the Gulf Coast of Florida. In 1904, John Cocoris arrived with his five brothers from Hydra in Greece. They had run a sponge business there and brought with them the latest technology: deep-sea diving suits. They revolutionized the sponge industry in Tarpon Springs and created a boom that was to last fifty years.

Within a year, fifteen hundred Greeks had also moved to Tarpon Springs. By 1940, almost half of the residents were Greek. Eventually, it became the only settlement in the country where a majority of people were Greek. Because they helped bring prosperity to all in the area, white and Black residents alike appreciated the Greek newcomers.

Greek American couples often worked together in small, family-run businesses. This woman is unloading loaves of crisp bread from the oven at a Tarpon Springs, Florida, family bakery in 1968.

## Why Greeks Stayed

Although life in the United States was hard and sometimes unpleasant, early Greek immigrants saw that there was more oppor- tunity here than in Greece. When they first left home, they had planned to return after mak- ing their fortunes. Some did go back, with or without money, but many more became used to the new land. They saved enough money to go into business for themselves and made good livings running restaurants, small shops, shoeshine parlors, or jewelry stores. Those who had skills in Greece, such as bakers and silver- smiths, put them to use in the United States as soon as they could. And as Greek women arrived from the homeland, the men gave up the idea of returning and settled in the States.

## The Men Were Lonely

In the early 1900s, only seven in every one hundred Greek immigrants were women, so the men lacked female companionship. They kept each oth- er company in the Greek cafes, sipping thick, dark coffee, the air heavy with smoke from cigars, cigarettes, and pipes. They shared their experiences of the day, talked about their families and villages back home, and argued about politics in Greece. They played

## WHERE THEY SETTLED

Greeks settled in "Greektowns" all over the U.S., usually sections of larger towns and cities such as Lowell, Massachusetts; Salt Lake City; Tarpon Springs, Florida; Chicago; St. Louis, Missouri; New York City; and towns on Long Island and throughout New York State. The most important cen- ter of Greek settlement was, and still is, New York City. The archbishop of the Greek Orthodox Church of North and South Amer- ica is based there. And the two main Greek- language papers, *Atlantis* and the *National Herald,* were based in New York, where the *National Herald* is still published today.

A typical Greek cafe on Washington Street in New York City in 1919. Notice the small cups of coffee, the pipe, the *bouzouki,* or Greek mandolin, and the fact that there are only men present. In the early 1900s, the overwhelming majority of Greek immigrants were men.

cards, listened to a *bouzouki* (Greek mandolin) player, and would cheer while belly dancers entertained them from time to time. The men sang and danced with each other. Sometimes, traveling performers put on a show, making shadows against a white sheet to tell the same old story of how a clever Greek got the better of a Turkish official.

The young bachelors who stayed in the United States wanted to settle down and marry after a while. Often, they would write letters to relatives in Greece — perhaps their father, perhaps a cousin — asking for help in finding a suitable wife. The relatives would send a picture of a young woman. Once the match was arranged, the "fiancée" made the journey over to the States. Women immigrating for arranged marriages were called "picture brides."

Usually the men married their picture brides, but sometimes a man changed his mind and refused to go through with the marriage. One man who tried this was sued by the cousin of the woman and had to pay all her expenses.

## Women Brought Home Life with Them

Whether they were brought over as picture brides to marry unknown men or followed to join their husbands, Greek women found their way over to North America in increasing numbers. By 1930, one in three Greeks in the United States was a woman.

The women were not educated and spoke little English. A few worked in the factories in the Northeast. When a husband started his own small business, the wife often worked with him. But generally, women were expected to recreate the home life they had all known in Greece: cooking traditional foods, preserving customs, raising children, establishing the church as the center of the community, observing holy days and celebrating birthdays.

Before Greek women arrived, home life for Greek men in America was quite simple. They shared cheap apartments and took turns staying home from work to cook and do housework. Typical dinners were hot dogs every day, with one other item, such as eggs, rice, or lentils. On Sundays, they might have meat, soup, and beer. With marriage came some of the stability of family life, but Greeks immigrants still missed the support of the extended family and community with which they had grown up in Greece.

## Dating and Marriage

Greek attitudes toward dating and marriage changed very little when they arrived in the United States. Greek American girls were kept at home under the watchful eyes of relatives. Greek American boys, who were expected to date, had to take out American girls. If a Greek American girl and boy wanted to date in the American way, they could only meet at church services and celebrations or at the girl's house with other people present. Naturally, secret meetings were arranged, but in small communities, they were hard to keep secret.

Greek American girls who were seen with different dates were not thought well of, and boys couldn't afford to be seen with the same girl more than a couple of times or everyone would be pushing them into an engagement. In this way, parents made it very hard for their Greek American children to marry within their community, even though the parents wanted them to.

As if the rules for dating weren't hard enough, the ones for marriage were even more difficult for Greek Americans to follow. American boys and girls decided for themselves whom they wanted to marry based on love and attraction. So the idea of marrying the person one was told to didn't go down too well with younger Greek Americans.

## And Then They Had Children

Unlike the large families their parents had had in Greece, Greek Americans tended to have just a couple of children. The family life they knew was otherwise much like the one they had left behind. Children had to study hard and follow strict dating rules, and they had to be home on time or else! Their parents assigned them duties around the house and yard but did not give them an allowance as a reward. The eldest son might take a job after school but in most cases had to turn his earnings over to the father to be included in the family income.

When it came to discipline, the mother would keep order in the house. If she was having trouble with a child, she would "tell father," who would deal harshly with the culprit. Children never told their parents if they got in trouble at school because they knew they would be punished again for the same thing at home. Discipline may have been strict by today's standards, but Greek American homes were rarely troubled by juvenile delinquency, and the families remained close.

## Improving Their Chances Through Education

Before World War I, one in four Greek immigrants was unable to read and write. Because they were busy working to survive, immigrant Greeks could rarely attend school themselves. They made sure, though, that their second-generation Greek American children were put through school. "Don't be like me, ignorant; learn English, be educated," said one mother to her children. Because the children could not speak English, they were sometimes first placed in classes for learning-challenged students, but they did not take long to catch up.

In educating their children so that they could be successful, the Greeks also made a problem for themselves. As the second-generation Greek Americans went to American schools, they started to question the values of their foreign-born parents. They protested the rules about dating and the way marriages were arranged. Many preferred to work as professionals, such as doctors and lawyers, rather than continue the family businesses and trades that their parents had worked so hard to develop.

Not only were the older Greeks worried that their children, educated in the American customs and language, would forget their own ways; they also thought contact with Americans would lead to marriage between mainstream Americans and Greek Americans. And that would make the families less Greek. Through four centuries of Turkish rule, the Greeks had managed to keep their own culture. They didn't want to lose it after only a few decades in the States.

## Should We Be Greek, or Should We Be American?

Greeks immigrants felt that more education in the Greek culture was the answer. "Teach the children the American ways so they can do better. And teach them their language and history so they stay Greek. That way, our children will be successful Greek Americans," they said.

## GRENGLISH

The first arrivals often did not learn much English, as they spent most of their time together speaking Greek. When they had children, the children would learn English in school and answer their parents in English when asked questions in Greek. One result was "Grenglish," a mixture of Greek and English. Words like *grosaria* (groceries), *gasolini* (gasoline), *caro* (car), *roofy* (roof), and *politsimanos* (policeman) became part of everyday speech in Greek American homes.

The traditional costumes worn by these young Greek Americans in 1947 are still worn today. They are evidence of strong cultural ties to the homeland; the flag behind the children shows Greek Americans' loyalty to the United States.

The new head of the Greek Orthodox Church, Archbishop Michael, is enthroned outside the Greek Cathedral of New York in 1949. Many Greek Americans feel that without the strong influence of the Church, Greek culture in America would have quickly eroded.

The communities and churches organized Sunday schools to teach the children about the beliefs and history of the Greek Orthodox Church. They also learned about the history of their ancestral country, about its dances, music, books, and religion.

For many second-generation Americans, maintaining their Greek identity also meant attending Greek afternoon school every day after public school. Like most kids, they would much rather have been playing. Instead, they sweated over subjects like Greek grammar, ancient Greek literature, national and church history, and geography.

The schools may not have been popular with the children, but they did keep the Greek heritage alive. Education was needed not only by the children, but also for new immigrants. Greek Americans naturally wanted to be accepted and welcomed in their new home, but the flood of immigrants that kept coming often created conflicts with other Americans. The newcomers did not

speak English, and many had no idea how other Americans expected them to behave. So a group of Greek businessmen founded the American Hellenic Educational Progressive Association in Atlanta, Georgia, in 1922. Its purpose was to help immigrants adjust to the American culture and learn the language.

Other Greeks felt that Greeks should stay Greek and not become Americans, so they formed their own associations to preserve Greek culture. And so the push and pull of becoming American while staying Greek continued in the early years.

## Staying in Touch

Even though most newly immigrated Greeks became more American with each passing day, they all maintained a strong interest in their homeland reading newspapers and keeping in touch with friends and relatives in Greece. Thirty thousand Greeks returned to Greece to help during the

Balkan Wars in 1912-13. More than any other issue at home, Greek American communities became involved with the political struggle in Greece between those who supported the king and those who wanted a parliamentary government. During the 1920s and 1930s, this division split Greek American communities as well. At least one Greek Orthodox priest, for instance, was fired because he did not support the same party as the majority of his congregation.

Despite these conflicts, the Greek American communities were held together by the things they had in common: They all had the same faith; they continued to celebrate and socialize together; and their schools, newspapers, and fraternal organizations all emphasized the same Greek identity and culture.

## Life in the Community

Like most ethnic groups in the United States, Greek communities grew into islands within the larger society where Greeks could be Greek, eating the food and speaking the language they were comfortable with. Women chatted from their windows and doors while the children played in the streets and alleys. The men argued in cafes and read the *Atlantis* paper for news of home.

Greek Americans formed hundreds of social clubs for people from their home towns and villages. In these communities, people dressed and spoke in familiar ways, and they all counted for something. They were proud and happy to be Greek. Above all, they had their own church.

Traditionally, the Greek community is based around its church, both spiritually and socially. It was the church that held people together through four hundred years of Turkish rule. The Greek Orthodox Church

### ESTABLISHING EARLY GREEK ORTHODOX CHURCHES IN AMERICA

The first Greek Orthodox services in Chicago were held in a warehouse in 1892. Within a year, the large Greek community there had built its own church and had had it blessed by a church official from Greece. In Brooklyn, rather than continue to use a Protestant church, the Greeks raised money to build their own, St. Constantine, which was completed in 1914. And so the story repeated itself around America: Wherever Greeks settled, they built churches.

was the backbone of the Byzantine Empire for a thousand years.

In the United States, it was the church that helped pull the community together. Its celebrations and forms of worship re-established the world the immigrants were used to. Greek families were expected to contribute whatever they could to their church. In turn, the church provided a place of worship, sometimes doubled as a school, and helped the down-and-out. Women formed organizations such as Philoptochos, meaning "friend of the poor." They would help those in the community whose need was greater than their own.

After a rough beginning and much sacrifice by the first three generations of Greeks in the United States, their families, communities, and customs became well established and accepted in the States. Greek Americans had fully adapted to conditions in their new homeland and at last began to enjoy the comfortable life that had been denied many of their ancestors.

These second-generation Greek American sisters are celebrating Christmas together with their husbands and children.  Only one of them married a Greek man, but they still remain a close-knit family following many Greek traditions.

# CHAPTER THREE

# FAMILY AND COMMUNITY
## GREEK INFLUENCE LIVES ON

**M**uch has changed over the years in Greek American families and communities. The individual men and women have become Americans, but with a difference. They have kept a strong sense of family and community, as well as their own cultural identity. In this way, they have what some Americans feel modern society is losing.

### Changes for Women and Men

A Greek of 1880 would never believe what the life of a Greek American woman today is like. For a start, she might work at a job outside her home. She dates men she likes and marries the one she feels is right for her. She no longer has to hope her father and brothers can make enough money for a dowry so she can marry, as she can earn her own money. She can say whatever she wishes about any subject, even when her husband is present. And she can do what she wants, instead of having to do whatever her husband demands.

That Greek of 1880 would probably think Greek American men of today had taken leave of their senses. Husbands do not feel bad about their wives working. They like having the extra money for the family to spend. They help out with the housework or looking after the kids and have even been known to cook up some tasty meals. In the old days, any Greek man seen doing these kinds of things would be the laughing stock of the community. His friends would say, "He is wearing a skirt."

One thing has not changed in most Greek American families, however: Men still control the family affairs. Many Greek

## A SMALL MINORITY IN A BIG COUNTRY

Today, about 1 million Americans of Greek descent live in the United States, almost all in large cities. About 160,000 Greek Americans live in New York City, with the largest single community in the Astoria area of Queens. Another 88,000 Greek Americans live in Chicago, and 76,000 live in the Boston area. The two states with the highest ratio of Greek Americans to the general population today are Massachusetts and New Hampshire.

Since 1528, when the first documented Greek immigrant set foot in America, more than seven hundred thousand Greeks have come into the country. Some of those returned to their homeland, but enough stayed and had children to create a Greek culture in America. Today, 25 percent of Greek Americans are first-generation Americans; 40 percent are second-generation; 25 percent are third-generation; and only 10 percent are fourth-generation Americans.

The young boys in this family portrait are dressed for a traditional dance. They are wearing costumes of the Kalymnian islands of Greece, which is where their great-grandparents came from a century ago.

American fathers are proud of the discipline they bring to the house. They feel it is the reason their children generally obey the law and rarely take drugs or become unmarried teen parents.

When Greek American women began working outside the home and sending their children to daycare centers, many older Greek Americans worried. They believed that a mother was meant to be at home, talking to the children in Greek and teaching them Greek ways while she cooked Greek food. How could she do this if she were at work?

The grandparents also worried about Greek Americans marrying someone who had no Greek ancestry. The children from these marriages were not always educated at Greek afternoon schools and did not always attend Greek Orthodox church. Without

these two important links to the homeland, how would Greek traditions and values be carried from one generation to the next?

The grandparents had good cause to worry, but the changes went on anyway, and they have not always been bad for Greek traditions. Fifty thousand non-Greek spouses have become a part of Greek American culture, including the Greek Orthodox Church, in an effort to understand or please their Greek spouse. And many of the younger generation who know little Greek still have a strong interest in Greek culture.

The church also applied pressure on Greek Americans to marry each other, requiring that a Greek Orthodox man or woman marry a baptized Christian who agreed to raise the couple's children in the Greek Orthodox faith. If these two conditions were not met, the Greek Orthodox person was no longer in good standing with the church. Despite these warnings, the number of interfaith marriages has increased greatly since 1980 to almost double the number of marriages between Greek Americans. Like other Americans whose ethnic identity is closely tied to a single religion, the children of these marriages maintain their ties to their Greek ancestry in many ways.

## Greater Freedom for Children

In Greek America today, not all children spend their free time studying at Greek afternoon school after public school. With so many other activities available, such as sports, attendance is dropping off at these schools. Even so, many six- to twelve-year-olds are still taken to Greek school by their parents. Pupils spend from one to three hours in school each day and get plenty of homework as well. Currently, four hundred Greek afternoon schools meet in the United States and enroll around twenty-seven thousand students. In addition, two dozen Greek American day schools enroll sixty-five hundred students, mainly from kindergarten to eighth grade.

## The Shrinking Family

Greek American families have generally become smaller

and less tightly knit over the years for three reasons. First, when Greeks came to the States, they still felt responsible for all their relatives. While they might only sponsor brothers coming to America, they still looked after the interests of more distant relatives. One man, for example, paid for the entire education of two nephews because he felt it was his duty. The hard life and poor conditions in Greece had kept families close so they could help each other. This was still true for the first immigrants in the United States. As Greek Americans became wealthier, they tended to become more independent of one another. The family may still include cousins, nephews, and uncles, but the idea

Two sisters get ready to play at a recital. Despite trends weakening the ties of Greek families in America, families are still close-knit and look out for each other.

## THE EVIL EYE

Greek Americans no longer seriously believe in the evil eye (a reputed power of some people to harm others just by looking at them) as a force affecting their lives, but they often continue the tradition of warding it off. A home is likely to have a large, blue model eye and a clove of garlic hanging in the kitchen, and both women and men sometimes wear small blue beads on necklaces or bracelets. These ornaments are meant to protect people from the evil eye.

that they all have to be looked after is not as strong as it used to be.

Secondly, Greek American families are having fewer children, perhaps two rather than a dozen as in the old days. Lastly, attitudes toward parents in their old age have also changed. Instead of being looked after at home, more and more aging parents are being placed in nursing homes, a trend shared by many American families. This is often upsetting to the parents, who worked hard to raise their children and expected to stay close to them and their grandchildren in their remaining years. Some grandparents who do not live with their children at home stay in Greek senior citizen residences and nursing homes run by Greek American communities.

## IMPROVED RELATIONS WITH OTHER AMERICANS

Over the years, as Greek Americans have settled into society and learned American ways, the negative image they had with other Americans during the first quarter of the twentieth century has largely disappeared.

The real turning point came with World War II. Greek Americans left the isolation of their communities to join the U.S. armed forces and mingled there with other Americans. At the same time, Americans saw how bravely the Greeks were fighting the Nazis who had invaded their country.

Asked their image of Greek Americans today, most Americans think of restaurant owners or Greek food. They think of family-centered lives, Greek weddings, and the Greek Orthodox Church. Some remember the Greek dancing they saw in the film *Zorba the Greek*. Some even think of long, unpronounceable names! But few, if any, negative ideas or images come to mind.

While official organizations provide one way for Greek Americans to meet, nothing beats the age-old custom of sitting outside shops or cafes in the cool of the shade for an hour or two of conversation with friends.

## Organizing the Community

While the Greek American family has tended to shrink over the years, this is not true of Greek American communities and societies, which have increased in size and number. Greek Americans' love for their home village or region is similar to American sports fans' love for their home teams. There are three hundred Greek American societies in North America, most of them dedicated to different regions of Greece. These societies allow Greek Americans with roots in the same region in Greece to stay in touch, enjoy time together, and trade information about their hometowns and villages.

The biggest Greek American organization, which is open to all Greeks, is the American Hellenic Educational Progressive Association. After it achieved its original purpose of helping Greeks adapt to North American culture, it concentrated on preserving Greek culture in North America. Today, there are over four hundred chapters around the country, with an active membership of fifty thousand and many more enrolled who do not participate in activities. Separate branches have been established for women (Daughters of Penelope), for boys (Sons of Pericles), and for girls (Maids of Athena).

Another major organization, the Greek Orthodox Ladies Philoptochos Society, began with several women's groups in New York working to help those in need in the Greek community at the beginning of the century. These groups combined into a national society in 1931, and there are 480 chapters in the United States and Canada today. They are the official charitable organization of the Greek Orthodox Church in America, working to preserve the religion,

A century ago, if a New Yorker wanted fresh flowers, he or she would often go to one of the small flower shops run by newly arrived Greek immigrants. Some Greek American families still provide this service today.

educate the young, and help Greek Americans in need, as well as Greeks around the world.

The local council that runs each church is the most important group in the Greek American community. It organizes the frequent festivals that provide local Greek Americans with dinners, dances, and religious and other celebrations. The council arranges activities such as scouting and baseball leagues. It raises funds for projects and charities and sponsors economic and business fairs. It runs the Sunday schools and Greek afternoon schools. The council really holds the Greek community together.

## Greek News Media

Few newspapers existed in Greece when the emigrants first left at the end of the 1800s because few Greeks could read. But in the United States, Greek immigrants learned to read and longed for news of their homeland. At least one hundred Greek-language newspapers came and went over the next century. The longest running is the *National Herald (Ethnikos Kyrix)*, which was first published in New York in 1915 and still prints all its news in Greek. Over a dozen papers for Greek Americans are published around the country now, most of them printed in English, as well as seventy-five radio and thirty television programs. These all help keep Greek Americans in touch with their homeland, their religion and culture, and American news that affects them.

Whatever changes have come their way over the generations, the Greek family and community are still going strong, providing support for Greek Americans and keeping the Greek heritage alive. If there is one organization most responsible for keeping the Greek family and community together, it is the Greek Orthodox Church.

A Greek Independence Day play is presented by students at William Spyropoulos School, a Greek school in Flushing, New York. The authentic costumes and use of Greek (note the date "March 25") demonstrate the value of Greek language and culture to the Greek American community

The interiors of Greek Orthodox churches burst with the rich colors of icons, murals, and paintings donated by church members. This church in Tarpon Springs was modeled after the Byzantine St. Sophia Cathedral built in Constantinople (present-day Istanbul, Turkey) during the Byzantine Empire.

# CHAPTER FOUR

# RELIGION AND CELEBRATIONS

## CORNERSTONE OF THE GREEK COMMUNITY

The Greeks have many old and magnificent church celebrations. One of the most memorable takes place on Easter weekend. On Holy Friday, a replica of the tomb of Jesus, covered with sweet smelling roses, lilies, and carnations, is laid out in the church. In some communities, thousands of people, each with a lighted candle, then follow the tomb as it is carried through the streets. The choir sings sad songs as the line of light snakes through the neighborhood. After everyone returns to the church, a service is held, and each person is given one of the flowers that were covering the tomb.

Just before midnight on Saturday, the congregation again fills the church for the service to commemorate the burial of Jesus. Everyone sits quietly in the dark until, finally, the priest lights the candles on the altar. He then lights a small candle which he passes to the congregation, and each person lights his or her own candle before passing it to the next person. The church becomes brighter and brighter until the golden icons on the walls glow with color. The people outside, who cannot fit into the church, light their candles, and the whole church sparkles like a jewel in the light of thousands of candles.

The choir of boys and girls sing ancient hymns without accompaniment. When they sing the Resurrection song "Christ Is Risen," the congregation lights sparklers, and, in some towns, fireworks are set off outside. Inside and out, explosions of light turn the night to day in a fiery crescendo that seems to lift the worshipers' souls to heaven.

The Easter service continues until two in the morning, and people are given red eggs as they leave. One legend about why the eggs are colored red says that a farm girl would not believe Jesus had risen from the dead unless the eggs in her basket turned red. They immediately became red, according to the story, and so she believed.

Church members return home with their eggs and eat soup before going to bed. They eat soup because it is easier to digest

---

### EASTER WITH A BANG

One Greek Orthodox parish, in Tarpon Springs, Florida, occasionally celebrates Easter with an extra bang. They explode bombs — harmlessly, of course — in a tradition developed on the Greek coast close to Turkey. Many of the congregation's ancestors came from the island of Kalymnos, where islanders used to set off bombs so the Turks could hear the explosions and know the Greeks were practicing their religion, even though they were still under Turkish rule.

Mass, an observance shared by Roman Catholics, is the central religious service attended regularly by members of the Greek Orthodox Church.

after fasting from sunrise to sunset for forty days, but the type of soup traditionally varies within each region of Greece.

## What Is the Greek Orthodox Church?

The Greek Orthodox Church was once part of the early Christian Church. While it has many similarities with the Roman Catholic Church, from which it separated 950 years ago, the Greek Orthodox Church strictly follows the original writings and teachings of the early Christian Church. Its prayers today are no different from those recited nearly two thousand years ago. The Greek Orthodox Church has close ties with the Russian Orthodox Church, both of which come from the ancient church of the Byzantine Empire. Although each has strong national interests, there has been talk of recombining both

religions into one Orthodox Church, as they used to be 550 years ago.

## Establishing the Church in America

Wherever a Greek American community grew, there was soon a Greek Orthodox church. When the Greeks came to the United States, they had no church buildings of their own and had to borrow the churches of other religions or hold services in any large building they could find. Over time, Greek communities raised money to build their own churches and hired (and fired) their own priests.

The first Greek Orthodox church in the United States was Holy Trinity in New Orleans, built in 1877 by a wealthy Greek family that had arrived before the main flood of immigrants. By 1923, there were 140 Greek Orthodox churches throughout the United States. Because the Greek

Orthodox authorities in Europe did not send priests to start parishes here, Greek American community councils controlled their local Greek Orthodox churches. To this day, parish finances, fundraising, building maintenance, church membership, and church organizations and clubs are not controlled by the priest, but by the community council. The priest only takes care of the religious services and other spiritual matters. Today, there are 450 Greek Orthodox churches in the United States, and almost every one has a Sunday school connected to it in which children are introduced to their religion. The Greek Orthodox Church is well established, with an archbishop in New York, a church newspaper with a circulation of 130,000, and a seminary in Brookline, Massachusetts, where priests are trained.

## ICONS

Icons are paintings, usually of saints, the Virgin Mary, or Jesus. They are the most common symbols in Greek Orthodoxy. They are found at home, in the workplace, and in the church. Icons themselves are not worshiped, but they help the faithful pray by providing an image of the figure they are praying to. Some Greek American sponge divers in Florida, for instance, keep a portrait of St. Nicholas, their patron saint, on their boat next to a small, lit lamp. Prayers are said by the captain, and divers are sure to make a sign of the cross before they slide into the water. At night, the crew lights candles to the Virgin Mary before going to bed.

When people come into a church, they often make a donation, light a candle, and place it under the picture of a saint. They are saying thanks for a prayer answered.

Having icons at home inspire the faithful to pray anytime without having to go to their church.

The sweet smell of incense helps make Greek Orthodox services a sensory experience as well as a spiritual one. In this picture, the incense is being used to help celebrate a baptism.

their sins. The smoke from the incense they burn stands for both their prayers rising to heaven and the answers coming back down. The many icons in the church are also symbols of the important religious figures they represent.

## Four Major Celebrations of the Year

Easter is the most important event in the Greek Orthodox calendar, as its elaborate celebration symbolizes. Holy Apostles' Day, on June 29, is another major event, commemorating the founders of the Christian Church, Saints Peter and Paul. Greeks observe Christmas in the same way it is observed throughout North America, with Christmas trees, Santa Claus, gift giving, and help for the needy. The fourth main event in the Greek Orthodox calendar is Epiphany, or Feast of Lights, on January 6. Epiphany celebrates the baptism of Jesus with the blessing of the waters for all sailors and a special ceremony called diving for the cross. It is the most important religious event for Greek Americans in Florida, where many families have traditionally made their living from the sea. The largest Epiphany celebration outside Greece is held in Tarpon Springs, Florida, where thousands of visitors come from around the world to witness and take part in the festivities.

The Greek Orthodox Church uses many symbols in its buildings, as well as in its services and daily life. Choir members in their robes, for instance, represent angels. A fountain represents cleanliness, where the faithful not only clean their faces, but wash away

The blessing of the seas in Tarpon Springs, Florida, at Epiphany, which takes place after Christmas. As he prepares to throw the cross into Spring Bayou, the archbishop is barely visible in the forest of banners and the throng of visitors, the media, and officials from all over the world.

All morning from dawn, the cathedral in Tarpon Springs glows with the light of many candles. Flowers, banners, and tall golden crosses are everywhere, as is the sweet smell of incense and basil (to commemorate one of the Greek Orthodox saints, Saint Basil). The choir sings in ancient Greek, and the service goes on until the afternoon. A basil branch is dipped into silver urns, and everyone is sprinkled with holy water as a way of blessing them. Then, in the courtyard outside, the archbishop makes a sign of the cross over a bowl of water that represents the oceans. He prays for calm seas and the safety of all sailors.

Everyone then lines up, starting with the altar boys carrying large, jeweled crosses of gold. The band and choir follow, then children in traditional costumes. A girl dressed in white carries a dove with blue ribbons attached to its feet. Next come members of various Greek American societies and organ-izations. The archbishop is dressed in dazzling robes of crimson, blue, and gold. Roman Catholic and Episcopalian priests and Lutheran ministers join the procession, to show the respect paid to members of the Greek Orthodox Church by their fellow Christians. The line of people winds its way to the nearby Spring Bayou (a small lake created when the tide comes in), singing slow, solemn music.

At the bayou, the archbishop reads prayers in Greek and the crowd answers him, also in Greek. The dove is released and then the archbishop hurls a cross into the water, where it sinks to the bottom. Young Greek men and boys dive to rescue the cross. The one who first reaches the cross returns it to the archbishop and, kneeling, is blessed by him and given a cross and chain of gold as a guarantee of good luck and happiness for the rest of the year.

Witnessed by thousands of onlookers, the cross is held high by the lucky teenager who managed to find it first in the murky waters of Spring Bayou in Tarpon Springs. As part of the January 6 celebration of Epiphany, the youth will receive the archbishop's blessing for happiness in the coming year.

Finally, the archbishop blesses the waters, a custom the Greeks share with many cultures, including the ancient Egyptians. A *glendi*, or party, then starts in the streets, with food, drink, singing, and dancing. The victorious diver is joined by successful divers from earlier years, and together they pass around silver trays to collect contributions for various charities.

The day ends with the formal Epiphany Ball, led by the victorious diver. The boys wear traditional white skirts and leggings, red vests, and caps. On their feet they have the same type of shoes the Greek soldiers wore in the war against the Turks. The girls wear colorful skirts and sashes, embroidered vests, and veils. For jewelry, they are decorated with strings of pearls and coins.

## First and Last Ceremonies of a Member's Life

The Greek Orthodox Church marks the beginning and end of each member's life with special ceremonies. Forty days after a baby is born, its mother and father take it to church to be blessed, just as Mary, mother of Jesus, is said to have taken him to the temple after forty days. The priest reads a prayer and, if the baby is a boy, carries him around the altar before returning him to his mother. If the baby is a girl, the priest takes her as far as the screen in front of the altar, since only males are allowed into the altar area.

Usually within the next year, the parents take the baby to church again for christening. This ceremony makes the baby a member of the Greek Orthodox Church.

The service follows many of the same procedures as other Christian baptisms or christenings. The naked baby first is daubed with oil as a blessing. Then he or she is quickly submerged three times in warm water, to be cleansed of the transgressions that the Church believes all humanity is born with. The priest then hands the baby to his or her godparents, who dry and dress the baby in christening clothes. The priest says a few prayers, and the baby takes its first communion, after which the priest asks the godparents to return the baby to its parents. A reception for the congregation follows the service.

In Greece, the godparents used to hand out small coins to the congregation to thank people for witnessing the christening. Nowadays, they hand out small brooches to

A Greek Orthodox baptism. The godparents and priest have rolled up their sleeves for dipping the baby in the water.

A priest makes the sign of the cross over a baby who is being baptized. Before the baptism takes place, the priest stands at the entrance to the church with the baby and parents and proclaims that the baby is about to be brought into the church for the first time.

pin on dresses or lapels, with the sign of the cross and the baby's and godparents' names recorded on them. For the next three Sundays, it is the duty of the godparents to take the baby to communion.

At the end of a church member's life, the Greeks have a simple way of saying good-bye. They hold a wake, at which friends and relatives come to pay their respects and talk among themselves about the deceased. Some of the women may still wail or cry loudly in the traditional fashion to express their sorrow at losing the person. The next day, there is a service in the church, at the end of which the priest and family members or friends speak about all the good things the person did while alive. The congregation then files past the coffin to pay its respects one last time. At the burial that follows, the priest sprinkles wine, oil, and ashes from the censer (in which incense is burned) into the grave. Finally, friends and family of the deceased go to dinner, usually at a restaurant.

## Fasting

Like many religions, the Greek Orthodox Church encourages its members to avoid some foods and concentrate on the spiritual side of life during certain parts of the year. These fasts, most of which last from sunrise to sunset, are held ten times a year. The shortest are one day long, and the longest last for almost seven weeks, just before Christmas, and the forty days of Lent before Easter.

When the Greek Orthodox fast, they avoid all animal products, which means no meat, fish, milk, cheese, and eggs. They are allowed to eat fruit, vegetables, grains, beans, and peas, and they have become very good at making tasty dishes with these foods.

In the tradition of other miraculous healing shrines around the world, crutches abandoned by people cured of their conditions have been left in the Taxiarchis shrine in Florida.

## Miracles in the Greek Orthodox Church

The Greek Orthodox Church, like the Catholic Church, has a history of miraculous healing and allows shrines to be dedicated to such miracles. One shrine in Tarpon Springs was built in 1944, following the recovery of a young boy, Steve Tsalickis, from what was thought to be a brain tumor. Fifteen doctors had come and gone, unable to help him. On his deathbed, Steve asked his mother to bring him the icon of Saint Taxiarchis. When she did, he started talking to an invisible person and then told his mother to build a shrine to Taxiarchis. He asked her twice before she promised. The next morning, to the surprise of everyone, especially his doctor, he awoke and said, "Taxiarchis cured me."

Steve made a complete recovery and went on to become a teacher. Today, he has retired from teaching and owns a restaurant in Tarpon Springs. Four years after Steve's miraculous recovery, his mother, who didn't have much money, managed to build a small chapel as a shrine to Taxiarchis. Many believers have visited the shrine, often in the hope that they, too, can be cured. Some

The weeping icon of St. Nicholas in Tarpon Springs was last observed to have wept on December 8, 1973. The icon stands near the front door of the church. As the faithful enter, they kiss the glass that covers the icon and then light a thin candle beside it.

claim they have been. Every year on November 8, the Holy Day of Saint Taxiarchis, priests from neighboring Greek churches perform a service during the morning. In the afternoon, everyone celebrates at a feast held for the Tsalickis family and their friends.

Weeping icons are another form of miracle that are accepted and interpreted by Greek Orthodox Church members and clergy. Several icons (paintings of religious figures such as Jesus and the saints) in the United States and other countries over the years have reportedly been seen with tears coming from the faces painted on the wood. They are said to be a bad omen, warning of earthquakes, wars, and revolutions. There are those who try to find physical explanations for the tears and others who say there are no tears. Although scientific tests were done in at least one case, the scientist would not make his findings known because he felt that, whatever the results, people would continue to believe that the tears were either real or fake.

## Religion Is a Way of Life

For Greek Americans, religion is not something that only goes on in church once a week. It is also a part of daily life, and

### CHANGING CUSTOMS WITHIN THE SANCTUARY

Earlier this century, it was not unusual for Greek Orthodox congregations to stand during services for as long as four hours, men on the right side of the aisle and women on the left. Worshipers still follow this practice in Greece and in Astoria, New York, where there are many older Greek Americans and new immigrants. But at other churches throughout the United States, the church provides pews to sit on, and men and women are allowed to sit together.

Greek Orthodox priests are often asked to bless things as a regular part of their role in the community. After buying an icon, for instance, a family may take it to a priest to be blessed. It is then used at work and in the house to offer prayers and thanks. And when new businesses or projects such as houses are started, they are also witnessed and blessed by the priest.

Church members often go to services every day, and every week there is something to celebrate. Each of the many saints, for instance, has a particular day dedicated to his or her memory. At Christmas and Easter, everyone goes to church. On other religious holidays, maybe half of the Greek Orthodox community attends church regularly.

Whether or not they attend regularly, 70 percent of all Greek Americans consider themselves religious and connected with their church. In one parish, the priest would regularly send the altar boys to the coffee shops to ask for donations from the men who were not at church on Sunday. The men wanted to support the church, even though they did not go to the services, and would always give generously.

Even though most Greek Americans are very loyal to their church, declining church attendance is taken seriously as a problem in most congregations. Many feel that the main reason attendance has dropped slightly in recent years is that, though more churches now use English in their services, some still use old Greek. This is, naturally enough, a hard language for most Greek Americans to understand. Where Greek is spoken, some of the younger Greek Americans have fallen away from the church, sometimes preferring other religions. The Episcopalian Church, whose beliefs and rituals are similar to those of Greek Orthodoxy, has simpler services that are held in English and thus appeals to Greek Americans.

On the other hand, more recent immigrants, as well as many older Greek Americans, prefer to keep the services in the old Greek they are used to. And so while there may not be a formal division within the Church, churches vary widely in their use of old Greek. In Astoria, New York, for example, the services are completely in Greek, because the parishioners there want it. In many churches in the Midwest and the West, services are almost completely in English. In some churches where Greek is spoken, the congregation is provided with translated books so members can follow the service, and this has proven successful in keeping members.

There is no doubt that church-run Greek afternoon schools strongly influence many Greek American children and are responsible for their continued attendance at church. The children study from one to three hours each weekday afternoon, usually in Greek, with one day devoted to religious study. As most parents rarely speak Greek at home anymore, the children have little other connection to their language.

Sunday schools also provide religious education in English. The church has asked that parents enroll their children, and many do. Some parents even drive up in their pajamas on Sunday morning, drop off the children, and then go back to bed! These people may not go to church themselves, but they do recognize that unless they educate their children in their religion and culture, the children may lose their Greek identity. It is therefore the church that is the key to preserving Greek culture in Greek American communities.

**Having already spent a day at public school, these children show a strong interest in their after-school studies at Greek school.**

This troupe of Greek American dancers represents their community at a festival featuring the dances of many nations.

# CHAPTER FIVE

# CUSTOMS, EXPRESSIONS, AND HOSPITALIY

## THE FIERY GREEK CHARACTER

"**H**ey, help me into this dress, will you, Nina? It's too tight around the waist," yelled Diana.

"Sure, how about losing some weight," joked Nina as she helped Diana button up her white dress.

"Who's seen that new boy from New York?" someone shouted.

"I have, and he's got the cutest . . ." Her words were drowned out by a shriek from the quiet girl in the corner who had been trying for ten minutes to sew a red tassel back onto her apron.

"Sounds like Dora's pricked her finger again," teased Rena.

The others giggled.

Most of them were dressed by now, with their black vests embroidered in gold, matching their thin, black shoes.

"Isn't this a drag, having to skip the last syrtos?" complained Diana.

"I think it's because Nikos didn't want a girl to lead. He must have talked to Alkis and decided to drop it," yelled Rena, above the noise of the boys arguing in the changing room next door.

Any other ideas were drowned out by the door bursting open as one of the boys, dressed in his white tights and skirt, came into the

wrong room. All the girls screamed at him, but he had already gone. It was the boy from New York.

"Wow, he is cute," said Dora, as she went back to sewing the tassel.

### A Revival of Tradition

The behind-the-scenes preparations for a traditional Greek dance performance are always full of bustle as last-minute adjustments are made. Such scenes are becoming more frequent as the younger generation of Greek

**The designs of the costumes worn by these young Greek Americans belong to the different regions their families came from in Greece.**

George Katsaros, shown here in 1995 at the age of 107, came to America in 1913. He is beloved as a composer and performer of taverna music, a type of Greek music named for the taverns throughout Greece and Turkey — and the Greek cafes in the United States — in which it was played. Taverna music has been likened to American blues for its personal and emotional style.

counterparts are often surprised to see that their American cousins know more about traditional Greek dances than they do.

For Greek American teenagers today, dance offers an opportunity to be involved in their culture in an interesting way that combines exercise, social life, beauty, and history. For many of them, dancing is far more exciting than learning to read or write Greek, and what's more, their parents and the church approve.

Greek dances are quite different from modern American dance styles. For a start, they are group dances in which everyone dances together. They have no set time limit. They have been known to last as long as three hours each, with dancers coming and going as they please.

Americans discovers the fun of learning traditional folk dances. There are over a hundred traditional Greek dance groups in the United States today. Some of these groups have traveled to Greece to study, where their Greek

The dances provide an opportunity for men, women, boys, and girls to show off their skills. Because Greek dancers form long lines instead of pairing off with partners, the embarrassment of asking someone to dance is not a problem, and everyone is welcome to join in.

There are two differences between Greek folk dancing in Greece and North America, both involving the role of girls. In Greece, the girls still do not lead and are limited to the easier dance steps. In the States, the girls are allowed to lead and do the harder steps, and they are no longer limited to the slower dances.

Dancers wear many styles of costume, each from different areas of Greece. Greek American dance groups spend about four hundred dollars on the materials to make each one. They import the more complicated embroidered work from Greece and make as much as possible in the United States, using the same patterns and materials (usually wool, cotton, silk, and linen) that Greeks have used since ancient times. These costumes are always worn for performances and occasionally for social get-togethers, but normally, when Greek Americans go to dances themselves, they do not wear traditional costumes.

The musical instruments used in the dances today include both modern and ancient Greek ones. The bagpipe and lyre (like a small harp) are used as well as the *bouzouki* (a stringed instrument similar to a mandolin) and violin. Music, song, dance, and wearing elaborate costumes are not only for the stage. They are part of many celebrations for Greek Americans. Weddings are a good example.

## The Happiest Moment in a Man and Woman's Life

Traditional Greek American weddings are often big affairs with hundreds of guests. Preparations for the day usually start with the

Contemporary Greek Orthodox weddings retain many of the customs and traditions that have been observed for centuries. One of these is the presence of white crowns, which signify the "royal" status of the bride and groom within their families.

groom having a haircut while his friends sing to him; meanwhile, the bride is serenaded by her friends while they help her dress. Then musicians play violins and mandolins as they lead the bride, groom, family, and friends through the streets from the bride's house to the church.

The candles held by the bride and groom in a Greek Orthodox ceremony signify many things to many people. To some, they represent the soul approaching God to thank Him for allowing the marriage to take place. To others, they symbolize the flame of youth.

The Greek Orthodox wedding ceremony has not changed for hundreds of years, except that the bride and groom no longer wear the traditional Greek clothes. The American tradition of a white wedding dress and a tuxedo have taken their place.

The service is similar to other Christian wedding ceremonies, but there are some differences. The priest blesses the rings by holding them against the foreheads of the bride and groom and making the sign of the cross with the rings three times. Each of the bridesmaids and groomsmen then switches the rings from the bridegroom to the bride and back, three times. These motions are done three times to represent God, Jesus Christ, and the Holy Spirit, the three figures of the Trinity in Greek Orthodoxy.

The bride and groom share wine from the same cup before the best man holds white crowns that look like halos above their heads to show they are king and queen in their family. The bride and groom then stand in front of

the altar and kiss the members of the congregation as they file past. The reception that follows goes on all afternoon and evening and can last until five in the morning. There is limitless food and nonstop dancing. At the end, traditional songs are sung in which the family of the bride grieves the loss of its daughter.

When Greek Americans put on lavish weddings, they are following a long tradition that has been adapted to modern circumstances. Greek weddings in the homeland were the happiest times in lives that were otherwise full of hard work and few rewards. They were the one time the Greeks allowed themselves to cut loose, with celebrating often going on for three days and nights.

Greek men always provided large dowries for their daughters' weddings. It was something they planned for from the day a daughter was born. However, when young Greek Americans were ready to marry, they no longer asked for dowries, because they were earning enough on their own to support a family.

At wedding receptions, it is customary for guests to join the bride and groom in a Greek dance. As each guest couple joins in, they kiss the bride and groom and then fling a wad of money into the air as a gift to help the bridal couple establish their home and prepare for their first child.

The need for dowries may have disappeared, but Greek American fathers still had the urge to provide something big to show their love for their daughters. The wedding and the shower (a party for giving presents to a woman about to be married) provided them with the ideal alternative to the dowry. The size of the extended Greek family and the close Greek community also made it necessary for Greek American fathers to organize large weddings.

If ever there is an occasion for an extravagant Greek meal, it is the wedding reception, with hundreds of guests, multiple courses, and side tables stacked with Greek pastries and appetizers.

## NEVER REFUSE THE HOSPITALITY OF A GREEK

Many Greek Americans consider it an insult if guests do not eat, as they seem to be rejecting their friendship. A social worker in Chicago once visited two Greek American women who offered her coffee and cakes.

The social worker refused their offer, as she always did on her home visits. She was never allowed back in the house, even though the women needed her help to improve their living conditions.

Even today, in order to include as many friends and relatives from the community as possible, weddings often end up with many bridesmaids and hundreds of guests.

Not all Greek American weddings are big, though. Sometimes the parents cannot afford an elaborate celebration. In these cases, unlike earlier generations who would rather go into debt than not put on a grand wedding, the young couple will put on a smaller wedding that they can afford.

### At the Table

Whether putting on a wedding feast or a simple dinner at home, Greek Americans always give the best they can. Guests are usually treated to generous meals as a sign of friendship, and anything less gives the idea that the hostess does not care enough about her guests to put on a good spread.

Greek Americans have kept their Greek cuisine alive in restaurants and homes where Greek American women have the time and training to make their traditional foods. From lemon-flavored chicken soup to their fresh Greek salads, the dishes are always tasty and prepared with care.

Although Greeks eat a lot of lamb and goat, many Greek restaurants in North America also offer beef because it is plentiful and Americans are more used to the taste. Almost all Greek main dishes have garlic in them and are cooked with olive oil. Fresh herbs, such as oregano, thyme, and parsley, are also used in many dishes and help create typically Greek flavors.

If you can, ask your parents for a night out at a local Greek restaurant, and try some of their dishes for yourself. If macaroni is one of your favorites, you would like *pastitsio,* which is macaroni baked with cheese and ground beef into a wonderful, creamy dish. *Moussaka* is another creamy dish, made with layers of eggplant, cheese, and ground beef. *Tiropita* is a cheese pie (called *spanakopita* when spinach is added), which is made with the thin

Lunch is served! A gyros sandwich followed by a choice of two types of *baklava.*

## MAKING YOUR OWN GREEK SALAD

This is a healthful, easy-to-make salad that will fill up four people. Greek Americans have added items like potato salad, shrimp, and anchovies, and they use vinegar instead of lemon juice. Whichever way looks best to you, try making the salad for your family one summer day when the ingredients are fresher and more available in supermarkets.

### Ingredients

1 large head romaine lettuce
12 sprigs watercress, if available
2 tomatoes, cut into wedges
1 cucumber, peeled and sliced
    into thin fingers
1 avocado, peeled and sliced
    into wedges
1 cup feta cheese, crumbled
1 green pepper, sliced into rings

4 canned red beets, sliced
12 Greek (kalamata) olives
12 pickled Greek salad peppers
4 radishes, sliced
4 green onions, halved lengthwise
1/2 cup lemon juice, squeezed fresh
1/2 cup olive oil
1/4 cup fresh oregano, finely chopped
    (or 2 teaspoons dried)

### Instructions

1. Line a large bowl with the outside lettuce leaves. Shred the remaining lettuce and place on top.
2. Layer the watercress and then the tomato wedges in the bowl, and place the cucumber fingers between the tomatoes. Then put the avocado wedges around the edge of the bowl.
3. Sprinkle with feta cheese, and then top with green pepper slices.
4. Next, put sliced red beets in the bowl, then arrange the remaining vegetables on top in an attractive pattern.
5. Drizzle lemon juice over the salad and then oil; lightly sprinkle with oregano.
6. Serve immediately, letting each person help himself or herself from the salad bowl. Accompany with toasted garlic bread.

## MAKING BAKLAVA

If you've ever looked at the many layers of baklava and wondered how on earth anyone made it, wonder no longer! It's not that hard, and it's well worth the effort. The secret is in properly treating the paper-thin filo dough, which you can buy in the freezer section of most supermarkets. Filo should be defrosted in the refrigerator and then left at room temperature to warm for a couple of hours. Leave the dough in its plastic wrapping until ready for use. And while working on the dough, keep it moistened with oil so it doesn't dry and crack.

What is hard to make is the filo dough itself, as it is so thin. In the old days, Greek women would mix flour, cornstarch and water into a dough and stretch it out over a bed with a sheet over it, or over a large table. They would keep stretching until the dough was the thinnest they could possibly make it.

The word *filo,* which is sometimes spelled "phyllo," means "leaf" in Greek; that gives an idea of how thin the pastry has to be made. Today, the beds have been replaced by machines, and you buy filo ready-made, so it is much easier to work with.

If you want the traditional recipe for baklava, use melted butter and shortening instead of canola oil; and use sugar dissolved in hot water for the syrup, instead of maple syrup.

### Ingredients

1 pound filo dough
1 cup canola oil (or a can of canola spray)
1 cup pecans, finely ground
1 cup pecans, chopped
1 cup blanched almonds, chopped
(blanched means skins removed)

1/2 cup crushed zwieback*
2 teaspoons cinnamon
2 cups maple syrup
1 tablespoon lemon juice
or 1 teaspoon vanilla

### Instructions

1. Preheat the oven to 350°F.
2. Open up the filo dough gently, and brush (or spray) oil over the top sheet and any exposed edges of lower sheets.
3. Brush or spray a fourteen by nine by three-inch baking dish with oil.
4. Place the top filo sheet into the pan, and brush the next sheet in the pile with oil.
5. Repeat step three until you have six sheets of pastry in the pan.
6. Mix the nuts, zwieback, and cinnamon and sprinkle half over the top sheet.
7. Put on two more sheets of oil-brushed filo.
8. Sprinkle a quarter of nut mixture on top.
9. Add another two sheets of brushed dough.
10. Sprinkle remaining nut mixture on top.
11. Add the last few sheets of dough, brushing each generously.
12. Fold the edges of the dough over the top of the baklava, and brush again with oil.
13. Sprinkle with drops of water to prevent the pastry from curling while baking.
14. Cut the baklava into one-inch squares and place pan in the oven for an hour.
15. Heat the honey or syrup and lemon juice and stir until mixed.
16. Check the baklava after thirty minutes, and remove when the top is a golden color.
17. Pour syrup mixture over the baklava, and let cool.
18. Serve when cold. The baklava will stay crispy and edible for a week or two at room temperature as long as it is not covered.

* Zwieback is an American addition that helps soak up the syrup. It can be found in the baby-food section of most supermarkets.

This baker is folding sheets of filo dough into the shape needed for triangular baklava. In any one day, she bakes two thousand pastries as well as eight hundred loaves of Greek bread, some of which can be seen in the oven behind her.

layers of crunchy filo pastry. *Tzatziki* is a vegetable dish made with cucumbers and a spiced sour cream and provides a cool and light snack on hot days. An interesting dish is *dolmades,* which is grape leaves stuffed with rice and ground meat, often with sweet currants and sour lime or lemon to provide a typically Mediterranean flavor.

For dessert, Greeks are particularly fond of *melomakaronas* (cookies made with orange juice and honey), *galaktobouriko* (egg custard), and of course, the delicate, crispy pastry *baklava,* for which they are famous.

## And with the Food, Some Traditional Drinks

Greek Americans drink the same beverages as other Americans, but they do like a few traditional drinks that come from Greece. Perhaps the most famous is *ouzo,* a Greek liqueur (a strong, alcoholic drink) that is anise flavored,

like licorice. Another favorite is a dry, white wine, called *retsina,* flavored with pine sap.

Coffee is commonly offered to visitors at home. It is made with very finely ground coffee beans. A lot of coffee is added to some water and sweetener in a small pot, and the

Syrup glistens on the baklava, making it look as good as it tastes. If you look closely, the layers of filo dough and nuts are visible.

Dancing is a social occasion at Greek festivities in which families and friends join together, literally. The snakes of dancers form circles or spirals as they move around the room. Often, the dancers stay in place, swaying to the energetic beat of the music.

mixture is heated until it almost boils. It is then poured into very small cups, because it is so strong and black.

## Any Excuse for a Party

Most Greek Americans like to celebrate together whenever they can. When they do, they have appetizers and drinks. They talk and sing. At more traditional celebrations, the violins and bouzoukis start up, and then everyone joins in the same dances Greeks have been doing for thousands of years.

Outdoor parties, called *glendi,* are a favorite, especially in the South and in the North during the summer. Glendi are often used as fundraisers for the church or charities and attract people with traditional Greek foods, music, and dancing.

Dinner and dance evenings are added to many religious days. They provide more opportunities to dress up and have a good time.

## Traditional Celebrations

Like most other Americans, Greeks in the United States observe holidays such as the Fourth of July, Halloween, Thanksgiving, and Christmas. Sometimes they add their own special foods, like pumpkin patties or olives and feta cheese to go with turkey and other traditional American holiday dishes.

They also celebrate a few distinctly Greek holidays. Greek Independence Day is celebrated on March 2, with a parade, speeches, dinner, and a dance. One community even brings over members of the Royal Guard from

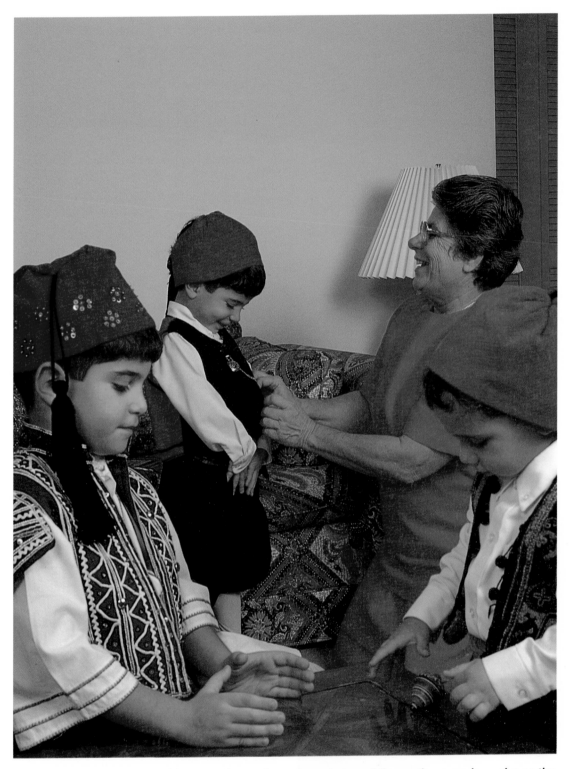

A grandmother helps one of her grandsons dress for a dance while another grandson shows the youngest how to play with a traditional Greek top.

## READING THE SIGNS

Like many people from Mediterranean cultures, Greek Americans use their arms and faces, as well as their tongues, to speak their mind. For example, if a person raises his head, eyes, and eyebrows to the ceiling, he means, "No, but you could persuade me if you continued." If at the same time, he raises both arms at the elbow, he means "Definitely not."

On the other hand, if he lowers his head, closes his eyes slightly and nods once, he means yes. If a Greek American raises his head, turns his mouth down and rubs his index finger along the side of his nose, watch out! It means he doesn't like you!

Athens, the capital of Greece, to head their parade. These men wear the traditional Royal Guard uniform with white tights, skirt, vest, and pompons on their shoes. They march slowly, raising their legs high in the air, and their performance causes much excitement for children and adults alike.

Greek Americans also celebrate "No" Day on October 28, the day the Greek government said it would not give in to the demands of the Fascists during World War II. Children dress up in national costumes, recite Greek poems, and sing patriotic songs to commemorate Greek courage.

## Traditional Customs

The custom of naming children after their grandparents is still used in Greek American households. The oldest son is named after his father's father, and the second son is given his mother's father's name. The oldest daughter is named after her mother's mother, and the next daughter is given her grandmother's name on her father's side. After that, parents name their children after dear friends, loved relatives who have died, or saints in the Greek Orthodox Church. A mother may pray to a particular saint and promise to name her child after that saint if she is guaranteed a healthy child, for instance.

One European custom that is not practiced much in the United States anymore is celebrating a birthday on the saint's day instead of on the anniversary of the birth. For instance, if a Greek boy named Nicholas were born on February 2, he would celebrate his birthday on the day St. Nicholas is celebrated in the church, which is December 6. Greek Ameri-

**Two children take turns reciting Greek poems on Greek Independence Day, which is celebrated every March 25.**

A winning combination: delicious food and a good laugh. Three sisters pass the pastitsio (macaroni baked with cheese and ground beef) while enjoying a joke at a family meal.

cans have an even better idea: They celebrate both days! The regular birthday is celebrated as usual, and the saint's day is celebrated with open houses in every home where someone is named after a saint.

## Greek American Humor

Just as Greek Americans appreciate American jokes because they understand the problems and realities the jokes are based on, they also have a special fondness for jokes based on the experiences of Greeks here and in Europe. Of course, a Greek joke that appeals to first-generation Greek Americans may be only slightly funny for second-generation Greek Americans, as this joke about Greeks and Italians illustrates: An Italian goes to Greece for a vacation and seeing some figs in a tree, climbs up and starts to eat some. The old lady who owns the tree yells at him to get down. Not understanding Greek, the Italian ignores her and keeps on eating. This upsets the old lady, who picks up a stone and hurls it at the man. It hits him on the head and knocks him unconscious to the ground. The old lady rushes up to him, and as she bends over him, he recovers consciousness and says "Aqua," which is Italian for "water." Hearing him say "Akoua" (which in Greek means "I heard") the old lady replies, "Well, if you heard, why didn't you get down?"

Whether they laugh at these jokes or not, Greek Americans have much to be happy about. They have come a long way in the last century, carving a place for themselves in the land of their dreams.

This diver has washed the sponges he has harvested from the sea floor and hung them around his boat to dry. He is one of a handful of sponge divers left in the United States.

# CHAPTER SIX

# CONTRIBUTIONS TO AMERICAN CULTURE

## FROM THE ALPHABET TO *ZORBA THE GREEK*

For many people in North America, the film *Zorba the Greek* was their first exposure to Greek culture. This movie helped popularize Greek dancing and music in the 1960s, and together with the hundred thousand Greek restaurants and fast-food establishments around the country, it has provided a taste of modern Greek culture in America. According to one survey, by the 1980s, one in two Americans had tasted Greek food, and one in four "liked it very much." Since then, the popularity of Greek food, especially as served in Greek American restaurants, has risen dramatically.

### Greek Food

When the first Greek restaurant, the Peloponnesos (named after the southern part of Greece) opened in Manhattan in 1857, many New Yorkers quickly fell for the taste of Greek food. But it was another fifty years before more Greek restaurants were established and most Americans had the opportunity to enjoy Greek cooking.

The Greeks who arrived at the turn of the century sold hot dogs and other food on the streets and so originated what we know today as fast-food eating. With the profits they made

There's a knack to eating gyros, a meal that is quick and popular — but sometimes messy. Opening wide and using lots of napkins helps! Greek Americans pioneered fast-food and "takeout" on the streets of Greek neighborhoods around the turn of the century.

**If long lines are any indication, this fast-food restaurant serving gyros and souvlaki has succeeded in convincing customers to make it their "Greek answer to McDonald's."**

In Chicago, for instance, Greek American food vendors sold snacks and sandwiches to factory workers from lunch wagons. When that was forbidden by the Chicago city government, Greek Americans combined forces and money to open regular restaurants. Despite coming under attack from newspapers and competitors, the Greeks kept going. (One competitor, determined to keep Greek Americans out of the food business, printed an advertisement for "John's Restaurant, Pure American. No Rats, No Greeks.") By 1913, Chicago boasted six hundred Greek-owned restaurants, giving rise to the saying that "when a Greek meets another Greek, they start a restaurant." Today, one in three eating places in Chicago alone is Greek owned. Although most fast-food restaurants in the United States are not Greek owned, the fast food industry can thank those Greek Americans and their lunch wagons who catered to busy workers eating on the run at the turn of the century.

A Greek sandwich that has stood the test of time in North America is the *gyros* (pronounced "HE-ros" or "JI-ros" and meaning "round" in Greek). It is made from ground beef and lamb that has been pressed into a cylinder shape, put on a spit, and roasted. The crispy outside is then sliced off in thin strips and placed on a thick pita bread with vegetables and yogurt sauce. Two other Greek

from these first "takeout" stands, they bought and ran their own restaurants and fast-food shops. At first, they served primarily fellow members of the Greek community, but soon they began catering to broader communities across the country.

favorites are listed on menus in many restaurants throughout the United States: For the health- or diet-conscious, Greek salads offer a choice when a light but filling meal is required; and for those with a sweet tooth, crispy Greek pastries like baklava are always a treat.

## An Ancient Legacy in a New World

Tasty though these dishes may be, they are just a small part of Greek contributions to U.S. culture. In fact, many aspects of life in the United States have their beginnings in ancient Greece. The ancient Greeks developed many of the science, arts, and humanities subjects that we study and use today, as well as some of the sports that we play and watch.

## Sports

The Olympic Games, or Olympiad, have been a part of American sports since they were revived in Athens, Greece, in 1896 (the games had been stopped by the Christian Church fifteen hundred years before because of their connection to pagan gods). Several U.S. cities have been selected to host the Olympics since then, including St. Louis in 1904, Los Angeles in 1932 and 1984, Lake Placid, New York, in 1980, and Atlanta, site of the Olympic centennial in 1996. Hundreds of millions of American spectators and viewers over the years have thrilled at the speed and skill of the international athletes who compete in the Olympics. Hundreds of Americans have known the surge of pride from par-

### THE CHARACTER OF THE OLYMPICS

The ancient Greeks considered the Olympics very serious contests that had to be won, even if the cost was death. In fact, the word *athlete* comes from *athlos,* which means a contest taking place in a stadium or on the battlefield. When they were first revived a hundred years ago, the Olympics were held as amateur events with no idea of financial reward; but recently, they have taken on the commercial character that they originally had two thousand years ago. Ancient Greek athletes were paid well with money and position when they won. One victor even got to marry the king's daughter and become the next king! Whether or not the revived tradition of Greek sports influenced the high stakes and finances of today's professional sports in America, they certainly established the trend.

**Milt Pappas, an outstanding pitcher for the Baltimore Orioles, strikes a classic pitching pose during spring training in Miami in 1959.**

Gus Triandos, shown here in Florida in 1964 during spring training with the Phillies, was a popular major league catcher for over a decade.

Athens to commemorate the soldier's run. Marathons have been a major American running event ever since. Cities such as Boston and New York host marathons that attract runners from all around the world.

There have been several noted Greek American sports figures over the years. Alex Karras was a defensive tackle for the Detroit Lions during the 1960s and was an All-Pro four times; he later moved into sports broadcasting and also won new fans for his parts in a dozen movies such as *Blazing Saddles* and *Babe*. In baseball, Milt Pappas pitched for the Baltimore Orioles from 1957 until 1973, and Gus Triandos was catcher for the Philadelphia Phillies from 1953 to 1965.

## Science, Mathematics, and Medicine

Many scientific terms, such as *physics* and *atom*, are Greek in origin and based on Greek discoveries. *Mathematics* is another Greek word and subject. The ancient Greeks established the principles of geometry and trigonometry and used them to estimate the distance to the Moon, as well as the motion of planets and the circumference of the Earth. The Greeks

ticipating in the games and the feeling of triumph as they won their gold, silver, and bronze medals.

The marathon that challenges so many runners today was originally run by a Greek soldier twenty-five hundred years ago, acting as a messenger for his general on the battlefield at Marathon in Greece. The marathon was created as a sport in the 1896 Olympics in

## SPORTS FROM THE ANCIENTS

The ancient Greeks developed many of the types of competition upon which modern sporting events are based, such as boxing, wrestling, foot racing, and discus and javelin throwing. Greek males could participate in up to three hundred sporting events a year, of which the Olympic games, started almost three thousand years ago, were the most famous. These games were so important to the Greeks that even wars were stopped so the games could go on. Cheating and bribery were unheard of as the games were a religious event, dedicated to their most important god, Zeus.

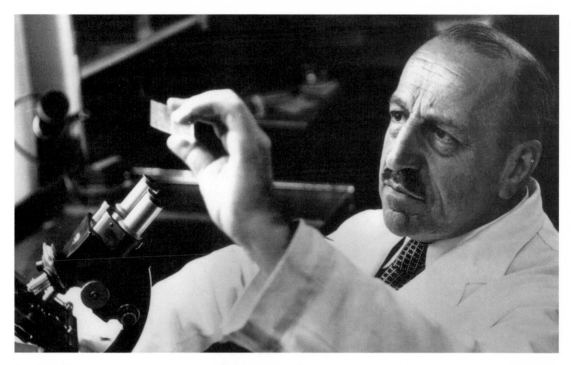

Dr. George Papanicolaou examines a slide at the Cornell University Medical School in 1958. His development of the pap smear, a test for cervical cancer, in the 1940s has saved thousands of women's lives.

also developed geology, identifying fossils as the remains of animals and plants that had died millions of years before. They studied rocks and minerals and linked volcanoes and earthquakes with land movement.

The ancient Greeks also made real advances in the field of medicine, and doctors today still take the Hippocratic oath, a code of conduct for physicians developed by Hippocrates, a Greek physician who lived twenty-four hundred years ago.

Greek Americans have contributed to medicine, too. The pap smear, a test that most women in the United States have on a regular basis to detect cervical cancer, is named after Dr. George Papanicolaou, who developed it in the early 1940s. Since then, the death rate in the United States of women from cervical cancer has dropped 70 percent. Another Greek American, Dr. George Kotzias, developed a

drug for Parkinson's disease that helps lessen the effects of this condition. Michael Aragnos made the Perkins Institution for the Blind in Boston into the world's leading school for people with impaired sight at the end of the nineteenth century.

## Serving Their Country

Perhaps the ancient Greeks' greatest contributions to North American culture are the political and justice systems they developed. Their ideas of justice and individual freedom are basic to democracy and strongly influenced the writers of the U.S. Constitution.

In the early years of their immigration from Greece, most Greek Americans did not involve themselves much with U.S. politics. There were exceptions, such as Lucas Miltiades Miller, who, in 1891, became the first Greek American elected to the House of Representatives.

ful farmer and landowner and didn't ask to be elected or even want to be, but his constituents insisted he represent them. Even earlier, Eustrate Delarof, a Greek Russian, was appointed the first governor of Russian Alaska in 1783 and helped bring order to communities there.

More recently, Greek Americans have become much more involved with politics: In the last quarter of the twentieth century, a dozen have been elected to Congress, including Olympia Bouchles Snowe of Maine in 1978, the youngest woman ever elected to the House of Representatives. Dozens have become mayors, including George Christopher, mayor of San Francisco from 1955 to 1964, who was born in Greece. Many Greek Americans have been elected state governors, and one of them, Michael Dukakis of Massachusetts, ran as the Democratic party's nominee for president in 1988. Spiro Agnew, whose father was Greek, served as vice president of the United States from 1968 until 1973.

In 1978, Olympia Bouchles Snowe was the youngest woman ever elected to the U.S. House of Representatives. In 1994, she was elected to the U.S. Senate, representing Maine.

He was a war orphan brought to the U.S. by a man identified as Colonel Miller of Oshkosh, Wisconsin, who had been fighting for the Greeks against the Turks during the Greek War of Independence. Lucas grew up as a success-

Greek Americans have fought in the armed forces since the American Civil War, when the first gunnery manual for the U.S. Navy was written by George Marshall, and George Colvocoresses commanded the USS *Saratoga*. Sixty thousand Greek Americans fought in World War I, and one of whom, George Dilboy, was awarded the Congressional Medal of Honor for his bravery. Greek Americans contributed $30 million to help fight that war and

Governor and presidential candidate Michael Dukakis of Massachusetts waves to his supporters at a political luncheon in 1988.

$200 million to fight World War II, in which thousands of Greek Americans also fought. One of them, Christos Karaberis, was awarded the Congressional Medal of Honor after he wiped out five enemy machine-gun nests, killing eight and capturing twenty-two German soldiers.

## Business: Sponges and Flower Shops

Greek Americans jumped into the United States. feet first and within months or years created the type of small businesses that helped make the U.S. strong economically. The first Greek American-owned small business, a flower shop, was established in New York in 1885. Through hard work and a shrewd sense of business, Greeks made a success of almost every business they started. Greek Americans tended to work in smaller shops and restaurants, although some have headed for big business, running large national and international corporations. Today, many Greek Americans work as lawyers, doctors, accountants, and teachers and in other professional occupations.

One product Greek Americans are especially known for making available to Americans is natural sponges. When a group of Floridians discovered sponges in the relatively shallow waters of the Gulf of Mexico at the beginning of the twentieth century, one of them invited a Greek American, John Cocoris, to visit and offer advice. The Greeks had dived for sponges in the Mediterranean Sea for twenty-five hundred years, passing on their skills from father to son. In those days, the Greeks had many uses for sponges, including lining soldiers' helmets. Cocoris saw that the Florida spongers were limited to working in water that was only thirty feet deep. They stayed in

Long a fixture in Florida's once-booming sponge industry, sponge boats have kept the distinctive lines and bright coloring that they acquired over the centuries in the Mediterranean. This boat bears the blue-and-white coloring of the Greek flag.

their boats and used glass-bottomed buckets to see through the surface ripples to the sponges below. They then hooked the sponges and hauled them to the surface with forty-foot poles.

Rather than merely offering advice, Cocoris went to the Greek Dodecanesean island chain off the coast of Turkey and returned with Greek sponge divers. Very soon, hundreds of Greek sponge divers arrived in Tarpon Springs, Florida. They brought with them the recently invented deep-sea diving suits that allowed divers to go underwater for hours at a stretch and reach the many sponge beds that lay up to 120 feet below the surface. Each suit had a helmet connected by a hose to a boat on the surface, so air could be pumped to the diver, allowing him to breathe underwater.

Even with the new diving suits, the work was dangerous. Above the water, there were storms and waterspouts. In the water, there

were sharks, moray eels, and rays with their stinging tails. An octopus might wrap its tentacles around the diver or his air valve, so the air being pumped in could not escape. The diving suit might then blow up like a balloon and shoot the diver to the surface, threatening him with a condition known as the bends (paralyzing cramps caused by coming up from deep water too fast). Divers would test themselves for the bends when they returned to the boat by smoking a cigarette: If it tasted bad, they knew they were getting the bends. While diving was dangerous work, it provided a living and was exciting. Divers would spend up to two months a year underwater in a world of exotic, colored fish, rock grottos, coral reefs, and all types of seaweed.

In the heyday of the Florida sponge industry, 180 boats were working the seas, staying out as long as two or three months at a time. Consequently, the little town of Tarpon Springs flourished as traders from all over North America came to buy the sponges. With so many sponges available and distributed to many parts of the country, most Americans were then able to buy and use them for a variety of household and personal uses.

Unfortunately, a red tide (the spreading of a red-colored, microscopic animal that lives in the sea and releases poisons that kill fish and other marine life) destroyed the sponge beds in the late 1940s, turning them into mush. At the same time, a chemical company invented synthetic sponges, which were much cheaper to produce than harvesting natural ones. The effect of both events wiped out the natural sponge industry.

In the years since, sponges have returned, but most of the boats have fallen out of use, and the men have moved to other professions. The community has survived by turning Tarpon Springs into a Sponge World, drawing tourists to the town not only for its Greek heritage, but for the history of the sponge industry and the beauty of the area. Today, as natural sponges have become popular again for cosmetic uses, a dozen sponging boats operating in Tarpon Springs are trying to keep pace with the demand from around the country.

## Ancient Greek in the Language We Speak Today

The English language includes many ancient Greek words such as *astronaut* (meaning sailor among the stars), *ecology, geography, architect, music, poetry, grammar*, and *cosmos*. Some American place names, such as *Philadelphia*, which means "brotherly love," and the fictional home of superman, *Metropolis*, are also Greek. The word *alphabet* is a combination of the first two letters of the Greek alphabet, *alpha* and *beta*. The Greeks developed the first modern alphabet, which used both vow-

### THE LAST DIVING-SUIT MAKER

Nick Toth, the last craftsperson to make deep-sea diving suits in the United States, learned from his grandfather how to make helmets out of copper, brass, and leather. He makes them now to sell to tourists in Tarpon Springs and for divers who need them to work in bridge construction and other underwater building trades.

els and consonants and evolved into the Roman alphabet we use today. American fraternities (groups for boys or men who join together for a common purpose) and sororities (the same kind of organization for girls or women), such as *Sigma Pi, Delta Gamma,* or *Pi Beta Phi,* all use letters of the Greek alphabet for their names. The use of Greek letters to identify fraternities and sororities is so common that these organizations and their members are known as "Greeks."

A few commercial products and some American military hardware and spacecraft use names from Greek mythology: For example, Nike shoe products are named after the Greek goddess of victory, and Ajax was a mythical warrior whose modern-day reward for his

Operatic singing sensation Maria Callas arrives at an international film festival in Venice, Italy, in 1956. Her career included film credits as well as singing success, and in 1987, ten years after her death, a group of friends made a cinematic tribute to her life called *Maria*.

With their close harmonies, snappy singing style, and hits like "Boogie Woogie Bugle Boy" and "Six Jerks in a Jeep," the Andrews Sisters, a trio of second-generation Greek American siblings, were wildly popular during World War II.

strength was to have cleaning products named after him. The superhuman feats of strength and daring of the mythical Greek heroes and gods make them appropriate names for the giant Hercules transport plane, the Poseidon missile, Titan rockets, and Apollo spacecraft.

One famous symbol in ancient Greece that is seen everywhere in North America — two snakes coiled around a winged staff, called a *caduceus* — was the symbol for the Greek god of medicine and healing, Asclepius. Today, it is used as the symbol of the medical profession in hospitals, on the sides of ambulances, and in medical literature.

The action/adventure books and movies that so many people enjoy today have their roots in early Greek literature, as do romance novels, with plots that have changed little over the last two thousand years. In modern times perhaps the best-known Greek American author is Nicholas Gage. He worked as an investigative reporter for the *Washington Post* and *New York Times* and has written several books. Two of his works, *Mafia USA* and *The Mafia Is Not an Equal Opportunity Employer,* helped expose organized crime in America during the 1970s. His book *Eleni* (1983) described his mother's capture, torture, and murder by rebels in 1948 during the Greek Civil War. The rebels wanted to take the children away from the village, and Nicholas's mother organized their escape. Young Nicholas got away, but his mother didn't, and his book tells the inspiring but tragic story of her life and death.

## Music

The ancient Greeks created the musical systems that developed into the major and minor scales (Do-Re-Mi-Fa-Sol-La-Ti-Do) that we are familiar with today. Much more recently, Dimitri Mitropoulos distinguished himself as a symphony conductor with the New York

Philharmonic during the 1950s. His memory was so good that he was able to conduct the orchestra without a score. In later years, he established a fund to help young American conductors become successful.

Maria Callas, a second-generation Greek American, performed with the New York Metropolitan Opera Company. Thought by many to be the world's leading soprano, she charmed many an opera lover with her beautiful voice before she died in 1977. The Andrews Sisters, Laverne, Maxine, and Patty, were also second-generation Greek Americans. They bolstered morale in the U.S. armed forces during World War II with their upbeat songs.

Tony Orlando, whose 1973 number-one hit song "Tie a Yellow Ribbon 'Round the Old Oak Tree" is the second-most-recorded song of the rock era, is also of Greek descent. Even today, tying a yellow ribbon around a tree or post has become a symbol in this country for welcoming someone home.

Tony Orlando and Dawn made "Tie a Yellow Ribbon 'Round the Old Oak Tree" a huge hit. Orlando is of Greek descent.

## Architecture and Art

The ancient Greeks built beautiful temples that have served as models for many American buildings. During the first half of the nineteenth century, the style was used widely in the design of museums, stock exchanges, banks, government buildings, and colleges. For most Americans, the most familiar building in this style is the U.S. Capitol in Washington, D.C., a city that is a showcase for Greek-inspired architecture.

Three Greek American painters — Jean Xceron, who worked in Paris in the 1920s before coming to the States, and William Bazioles and Theodoros Stamos, who were born in the United States — helped bring the abstract painting movement to North America during the first half of the twentieth century. Their version of abstract expressionism directed art away from copying the world exactly as it is. By the 1950s, abstract expressionist techniques of portraying people, things, and ideas as shapes and patterns had become widely accepted as an authentic American painting style.

## Drama and Film

The ancient Greeks created the idea of actors on a stage playing out a story. The basics they developed are still in use today, from Broadway to Hollywood. One highly talented Greek American writer-director — Elia Kazan — continued the traditions of his ancestors. He directed such Broadway plays as *A Streetcar Named Desire*, *Death of a Salesman*, and *Cat on a Hot Tin Roof*. He went on to make films such as *Gentleman's Agreement* (1947), which won an Academy Award, and write novels such as *America America* (1962) and *The Arrangement* (1967).

There is no shortage of Greek American actors on today's movie and television screens. Probably the most famous is Telly Savalas, who starred with his brother George as the bald, lollipop-sucking detective in the long-running "Kojak" TV series of the 1970s. One of his best-known expressions — "Who loves ya, baby?" — still crops up in general speech. Savalas also starred in over forty movies such as *Battle of the Bulge* (1965), *The Dirty Dozen* (1967), and *Kelly's Heroes* (1970), usually playing the hard-nosed cop or bad guy.

John Cassavetes directed a dozen and acted in two dozen movies from the 1950s to 1970s, including *Rosemary's Baby* (1968) and *The Dirty Dozen*. As a director, Cassavetes pioneered the method of allowing the actors to make up the dialogue as the film was shot.

Other Greek American film actors include Katina Paxinou, who won an Oscar as best supporting actress in *For Whom the Bell Tolls* (1943). George Chakiris played in a dozen movies, including *West Side Story*, for which he won an Oscar as best supporting actor in 1961. George Maharis starred in the famed television show "Route 66," for which he received an Emmy award in 1962. He has played in half a dozen movies since, including the fantasy *Sword and the Sorcerer* (1982). Olympia Dukakis has acted in several movies, including *Steel Magnolias* (1989), *Look Who's Talking* (1989), and *Moonstruck* (1987), for which she won an Oscar. Valeria Golino has recently brought her talents as both a dramatic and comic actress to the screen in such movies as *Rain Man* (1988), *Big-Top Pee-Wee* (1988), *Hot Shots* (1991), and *Hot Shots Part Deux* (1993).

Though not widely known today, one family name stands out in the history of American movie theaters: the Skouras brothers — Charles, George, and Spyros — who arrived penniless in the United States in 1908. They worked in restaurants while Spyros went to

Telly Savalas, shown here with his family, was for decades one of America's most versatile and beloved "tough guy" actors. Probably his best-known character was the tough but lovable Kojak. Kojak was reportedly originally conceived as a cop of Polish descent, but he became a Greek American when Savalas signed on for the role.

night school to study English and business. By 1914, they had saved enough to invest in their first movie theater, the Olympia, and within twenty years, they owned four hundred theaters around the country. In 1942, Spyros was also appointed president of Twentieth Century Fox. It was in one of their St. Louis theaters that the first precision dancing team, the Missouri Rockets, was born. These dancers were the forerunners of the renowned Radio City Music Hall Rockettes in New York City.

At the same time, another Greek American, Alexander Pantages, ran eighty movie theaters on the West Coast. Pantages had worked the Klondike gold rush as a young man but lost his money in a card game. He then made a fortune providing the miners with comedy skits and other entertainment, such as singing, dancing, acrobatics, and performing animal acts. When he moved to Seattle, he bought his first theater and added movies to his entertainment shows.

## A Century of Success and Identity

Within a little over one hundred years of arriving in the United States, Greeks have turned themselves into valuable members of society. At the same time, they have kept their traditions and culture alive. Despite much hardship and prejudice, they survived the early years. They formed tight-knit communities that have provided moral and financial support for their members.

The Greek Orthodox Church and afternoon schools continue to teach Greek religion, language, and social customs. Young Greek Americans, like others who value the culture of their ancestors, face competing attractions in the culture they live in every day, such as sports and activities with friends. Yet Greek Americans of every age appreciate the beauty and importance of their ethnic language and culture.

Olympia Dukakis holds up the Oscar she won for best supporting actress for her performance in the film *Moonstruck.*

For earlier generations, recent arrivals from Greece kept reinforcing Greek customs and traditions in Greek American communities. But this influence can no longer be taken for granted, as life in Greece is also changing. Fewer people in Greece are going to church, and the community spirit is slowly eroding as more families leave their villages and move into big cities. As Greeks in North America have discovered, keeping traditions alive in the modern world requires special effort. Greek restaurants and traditional folk dancing are just two of the ways that Greek Americans have maintained a lively interest in their roots while awakening other Americans to the pleasures and passions of Greek culture. From medicine to politics to movies, Greek Americans today enrich American life with their ideas, talents, and values, just as their ancestors have for the last century.

# CHRONOLOGY

**753 B.C.** The first Olympic Games are held in honor of the Greek god Zeus.

**510 B.C.** The first democratic governments are created in Athens and Sparta.

**400 B.C.** Democritus realizes the world is made of atoms; the first university, The Academy, is started by Plato in Athens.

**200 B.C.** Aristarchus realizes that the earth revolves around the sun.

**A.D. 1453** The Greeks are conquered by the Ottoman Turks.

**1492** The first Greek is said to arrive in the Americas with Christopher Columbus.

**1528** The first landing of a Greek in America is recorded; he is taken by American Indians and never heard from again.

**1592** Juan de Fuca, a Greek, discovers the waterway that will bear his name — the Fuca Strait — between what are today the state of Washington and the Canadian province of British Columbia.

**1652** The first Greek cafe in North America is established in New England by a Greek named Konopios.

**1725** The General Assembly of colonial Maryland declares Michael Youris, a Greek, to be a naturalized citizen, the first official Greek American.

**1768** Four hundred Greeks arrive in New Smyrna, Florida; in 1777, residents of this community move to St. Augustine, Florida, and establish the first Greek school and Greek Orthodox chapel in North America.

**1783** Eustrate Delarof, a Greek Russian, settles in Alaska to supervise Russian trading; he becomes governor of Kodiak Island.

**1787** John Paradise, a Greek scholar, marries into the Ludwell family of Virginia; he had met Benjamin Franklin and Thomas Jefferson in Europe and was persuaded by them to emigrate to the United States.

**1799** The first marriage between two Greek Americans takes place in New Orleans.

**1832** Greeks gain their independence from Turkey.

**1857** The first Greek American restaurant, Peloponnesos, opens in Manhattan, New York.

**1863** Captain George Colvokoressis commands the *USS Saratoga* in the Civil War.

**1875** Christos Tsakonas leaves for the United States with five friends; his account of his experiences makes the United States a popular place for Greeks to work.

**1877** The first Greek Orthodox church is completed, in New Orleans.

**1880s** The first major wave of Greek immigrants arrives in the United States.

**1885** The first Greek-owned store, a flower shop, opens in New York City.

**1891** Lucas Miltiades Miller of Wisconsin is elected to the U.S. House of Representatives.

**1892** The first Greek-language newspaper, *Neos Cosmos (New World),* is printed in Boston.

**1905** John Cocoris helps establish the sponge industry in Tarpon Springs, Florida.

**1907** The first Greek American school is established in Boston, Massachusetts.

**1912** Thirty thousand Greek Americans leave the United States to help Greece during the Balkan War.

**1915** The *National Herald,* a Greek-language daily newspaper, begins publication.

**1922** The American Hellenic Educational Progressive Association is formed in Atlanta, Georgia.

**1931** The Greek Orthodox Ladies' Philoptochos Society is formed in New York.

**1930s** The Skouras brothers and Alexander Pantages open nearly five hundred movie theaters, bringing the movies to millions of Americans throughout the U.S.

**1940s** With their upbeat songs and dynamic singing style, the Andrews Sisters bring cheer to civilian audiences and U.S. forces during World War II.

**1968** Spiro T. Agnew is elected Vice President of the United States.

**1973** "Tie a Yellow Ribbon 'Round the Old Oak Tree," first released by Tony Orlando and Dawn, hits the top of the charts; over the years, it will become the second-most-recorded song in the history of rock music.

**1973** The television show "Kojak" begins, starring Telly and George Savalas.

**1988** Michael Dukakis runs for president as the nominee of the Democratic party.

**1996** The Centennial of the Olympic games is held in Atlanta, Georgia.

# GLOSSARY

**Baba**  Greek for father.

**The bends**  Paralyzing cramps caused by coming up too quickly from deep water.

**Bouzouki**  A stringed instrument like a mandolin, used in Greek folk music.

**Byzantine Empire**  The eastern half of the Roman Empire; a Greek culture based in Byzantium in modern-day Turkey. It continued in power until 1453, when it was overcome by the Turks.

**Dark Ages**  In Europe, the period from about A.D. 476 to the year 1000 when learning, science, and the arts were not encouraged.

**Dowry**  Money or property that a woman brings to her husband when she marries him. Dowries are no longer in general use in the United States.

**Drachma**  A unit of Greek money worth about three U.S. cents.

**Evil eye**  The power some people are believed to have to bring bad luck to others just by looking at them or casting spells

**Glendis**  Literally, "fun"; an outside celebration with refreshments, Greek music, and dancing.

**Hellenic**  Of or related to the Greeks. The ancient Greeks called themselves Hellenes. The Romans were the first to call the Hellenes Greeks.

**Hymn**  A song praising God.

**Kafenio**  A coffee house in Greece for men only where they could go to dance and be entertained.

**Lyre**  An ancient Greek musical instrument like a small harp. It is still used today but now looks more like a narrow violin.

**Matchmaker**  An old woman who arranged marriages in Greece. She would meet with the fathers of the couple, who would decide whether the marriage should take place.

| | |
|---|---|
| **Modes** | (and major or minor scales) A system for arranging sounds in music with fixed distances between each note. *Do, re,* and *mi,* for instance, are the first three notes in the eight-note scale used today. |
| **Narghile** | Prounced NAR-geh-lee; a Turkish tobacco pipe that filters the smoke through a bowl of water. |
| **Orthodox** | (as in Greek Orthodox Church) The Eastern Christian Church, which claims to follow the original teachings of Jesus, without the interpretations of the Roman Catholic Church. |
| **Padrone System** | A system for bringing immigrants to the United States and finding work for them. The padrone would keep the immigrants' wages for a year as payment. |
| **Pedektos** | A lively style of Greek folk dancing with many hops and jumps. |
| **Red Tide** | An influx of red-colored, microscopic animals that live in the sea and release poisons that kill fish and other life. |
| **Resurrection** | The rising of Jesus from the dead, according to Christian belief. |
| **Syrtos** | A style of Greek folk dance with slow and dragging steps. |
| **Yaya** | Greek for grandmother. |

# FURTHER READING

Arnold, Frances. *Greece.* Chatham: Raintree Steck-Vaughn, 1992.

Burrell, Roy. *The Greeks.* New York: Oxford University Press, 1990.

Descamps-Lequime, Sophie and Vernerey, Denise. *The Ancient Greeks: In the Land of the Gods.* Highland Park: Millbrook Press, 1992.

Ling, Roger. *The Greek World.* New York: Peter Bedrick Books, 1990.

Manos, Dimitri. *The Greek Americans.* New York: Chelsea House, 1988.

Nardo, Don. *Ancient Greece.* San Diego: Lucent Books, 1994.

Odijk, Pamela. *The Greeks.* Morristown: Silver Burdett Press, 1989.

Scourby, Alice. *The Greek Americans.* Boston: Twayne Publishers, 1984.

Williams, A. Susan. *The Greeks.* New York: Thomson Learning, 1993.

# INDEX